HISTORY OF FASHIONS

HISTORY OF FASHIONS

ROSANA PISTOLESE
Director, Accademia di Costume e di Moda
Rome, Italy

RUTH HORSTING
Associate Professor of Art
University of California, Davis

JOHN WILEY & SONS, INC.
New York   London   Sydney   Toronto

Cover Photo *French costumes c 1690. A fan with a painting of a ball in qouache. Leloir, "Histoire du Costume," Ernst, Paris.*

Frontispiece *This reproduction from a painting of archers from paleolithic times appears extraordinarily contemporary in taste and style. Foto Mercurio.*

Library of Congress Catalog Card Number: 70-107591
SBN 471 69040 6

Printed in the United States of America

10 9 8 7 6 5 4 3 2 1

Preface

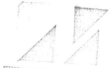
The evolution, the revolutions, and the religions and philosophies through which all civilizations have passed mark the brilliant ascent of human progress. The first forms of attire that the people of antiquity found convenient became accepted conventions by successive generations and gradually helped to establish the morals of costume and life. For, as Anatole France has said, "The morals are not only the sum of the biases of a community, but rather the creation of the civilization."

The costume, considered as a manner of clothing, represents the distinctive character of a country, of an epoch, of a personage; and always it mirrors the vicissitudes of human civilization. Through research of painting and other art forms, we can discover in traditional phenomena the contribution of clothing to human comportment, and vice versa. These historical revelations allow us to establish dialectically the reason for certain choices and to understand how the choice—the expression of taste and values—constitutes a mode of communication.

v

The costume always expresses the character of the person who wears it (or the intuition of the artist who portrays him); so we can say that the costume is the common esthetic form which man assumes throughout the ages, and it appears as a confession of humanity to history. Thus the costume elevates itself from a form of communication to an expression of values and transforms the information into a norm of social behavior, revealing the uniqueness of each society.

We have sought in this book to portray the general character of the costume in each epoch according to the art, the culture, and the society that have determined it. We have consciously attempted to illustrate each period by reproducing appropriate works from the greatest art available, for we believe that whoever designs and creates costumes must look to the ideals of other societies and must seek to capture their motifs in order to recreate them into new and different images.

The illustrations selected are representative examples of the history of fashions. The legends contain those details of costume that we seem to pass over lightly in the text only because we have chosen to maintain a fluent discourse; we wish the student to become fascinated with the subject and the layman to read this book with comprehension and pleasure.

Deliberately, we have often used foreign names for the different elements of costume, according to their national origins; the special terminology of costume *must* be known by people working in this field, whether it be in fashion or the theater. As the *History of Fashions* teaches, the study of costume developed especially in France and Italy; and in those countries, earlier than in other places, serious books were written which created a large, universally accepted vocabulary of costume, from which we still draw information.

With this book, we hope to stimulate student interest and scholarly research in all fields of fashion. The study of historical costume constitutes an irreplaceable element in the interpretation of theatrical costume, in the creation of contemporary fashion, and in the sociological understanding of an era.

Rome Italy
Davis, California
April, 1970

Rosana Pistolese
Ruth Horsting

Elmer Tolsted
Davis, California
April, 1961

Contents

Contents

Mesopotamia

Books about the history of costume present only a fragmentary documentation of all that humanity has conceived and really lived during the last five thousand years. In the face of the marvelous archaeological discoveries, we must often remain astonished at the very elevated level of taste and the modern-appearing fantasy of the old civilizations. For its surprising forms of evolution and because of our incomplete knowledge, the old world appears to us ever richer and more attractive.

As facial expression helped to convey the full meaning of the first words of man, so the costume is a complementary language through which men of all epochs have expressed themselves and have revealed to us their manner of life (Figure 1).

Between 4500 and 4000 B.C., our Western Civilization had its beginning in the two great river valleys of the Near East: the Nile in Egypt and the Tigris–Euphrates in Mesopotamia. There, ancient Oriental civilizations evolved as the result of centuries of tribal wars; conquest welded small groups of primitive peoples into the first city-states. These were organized for military efficacy and were dominated by religious

Figure 1. *Feminine statuette from Tortosa wearing a short, tight skirt and conical hat. Louvre, Paris.*

supernaturalism. But in them we also find the beginnings of a civil society. The new states coded laws for the protection of citizens and property, divided labor—thus creating the first industries—and even fostered the arts.

THE SUMERIANS

The Sumerian civilization is one of the oldest known, and from it stemmed other great civilizations such as the Babylonian, the Assyrian, the Phoenician, and many others, large and small, which developed in that area west of India and Afghanistan and south of the Black Sea. The language of those peoples derived, in a certain sense, from the Sumerians, who invented the art of writing. The Sumerian cuneiform characters were used phonetically in the Semitic–Akkadian languages until 3000 B.C. And still, during the first milennium B.C. the scribes collected texts and copied them diligently in the Sumerian language which had been extinct as a spoken language for centuries. Because language is a vehicle of communication, the costumes of those populations developed along parallel lines; the slight variations occurred because of differences in climate and the way of life. Those cultures were adaptations of the older Sumerian culture to varied environments, and they offered possibilities for new developments in industry and urban organization.

From rare examples of their costume, we are able to deduce that the Sumerians were a refined, slender, and elegant people who took extremely good care of their person and attire.

Both men and women wore plain but finely woven tunics, which the women usually draped over the left shoulder. Slaves of both sexes were naked above the waist, but their skirts often were multitiered fringes or petal-shaped pieces of cloth.

2

Men wore shallow, bowl-shaped hats, and women embellished these for themselves by adding coiled decorations. For the male of this period, long beards and long hair were elements of refinement. Finally, women sometimes created dresses by employing a unique *volant* wrapped spirally around the entire figure, up to the neck (Figure 2).

Between 1920 and 1930, the archaeologist C. Leonard Wooley found in the tomb of Queen Shubad in Sumeria unexpected and extremely interesting objects: precious jewels, diadems of gold, ornamental and very long necklaces, a small box in malachite for cosmetics, and other articles for the toilette. In the excavations of Ur, many stylized sculptures of fantastic, sacred animals were found (Plate 1). These are exceptionally well conceived and, for all their six thousand years of age, they are very modern in spirit and taste.

Figure 2. Sumerian cylinder seal, c. 1900 B.C. The cone-shaped hats of the women and the man's bowl-shaped hat are readily seen. The tunic was fixed on the left shoulder, and on the third figure from the left we see the characteristic spiral movement of the draping. British Museum, London; Art Reference Bureau.

Mesopotamia

3

THE BABYLONIANS AND ASSYRIANS

In 2450 B.C., the dynasty of Akkad arose. Sargon and his successors extended their conquests and imposed dominion on the rival cities of Mesopotamia. Sargon can be considered the prototype of all the great conquerors who have fascinated the popular imagination. He became a hero and was celebrated in legends and epic poetry one thousand years after his empire was extinct.

In 2100 B.C., Sumerian kings again united the cities of Sumer and Akkad and established internal peace and security for foreign traffic. They reconstructed a large part of the empire that Sargon had created and founded new cities such as Damascus. But before long, that empire also collapsed, and the ruling class of Sumerians was extinguished.

About 1800 B.C. an Amorite dynasty, dominating Akkad, reunited Sumer and Akkad into one kingdom which, from that time, was called Babylonia. Hammurabi, a great king of Babylon, is well known to us today for his codification of laws which were compiled and engraved on a stone column. The plundering of the Hittites and Kassites weakened the empire until it collapsed in 1500 B.C. Babylonian power was briefly revived under Nebuchadnezzar, but after other invasions, Babylon fell before Assyrian might (Figures 3, 4).

Between the Ninth and the Seventh Centuries B.C., the Assyrians created a true military empire, dominating all of the ancient Near East. In Ninevah, one of their great capitals, they gathered the plunder of their conquests, the treasures of the ancient world. Although they are known chiefly for their warring fierceness, the Assyrians also were civilized enough to create a great library of thousands of clay tablets.

A large number of well-preserved bas-reliefs record for us the principal aspects of these civilizations and even some particular ornaments differentiating the ranks of their citizens;

Figure 3. Hammurabi receiving the laws for his people from the sun god. Upper part of stele on which the Code is inscribed. Louvre, Paris.

History of Fashions

Figure 4. Bas-relief on a boundary stone from the Eighth Century B.C. showing Merodach granting land to a vassal in Sumeria. These costumes appear extremely simple, but the common motif of the apron probably signified a particular ceremonial dress; their shoes appear strangely modern. Louvre, Paris.

Figure 5. Bas-relief showing the typical costume with wings of Assyrian-Babylonian priests. Characteristic are the tunic with stole, the hair and beard braided and curled, the huge and elaborate earring. This relief reveals an evident knowledge of anatomy in its realistic interpretation of the human figure. Notable are the sandals covering the heel. From the Palace of Ashurnasirpal at Nimrud, Ninth Century B.C.; British Museum, London.

the priest, for example, is identified by a characteristic winged costume (Figure 5). The priest was a powerful figure for there were many gods to appease in Mesopotamian religions. In these old civilizations, we find no traces of the theater; the religious rite constituted the sole type of dramatic presentation (Figure 6).

In contrast to the rigid and geometric Sumerian models, Assyrian sculpture shows an interest in anatomy and realism; the life of the court, the hunter, and the soldier are depicted in great detail, and even the background plays an important role. Assyrian art is well preserved and brings us a faithful report of the customs, as well as the costumes.

The Babylonians and Assyrians made ample use of fashions which seem to be derived from the feminine costume of Sumeria; that is, with a similar spiral movement, they draped a long, horizontally fringed stole around the body. Persons of lesser rank wore a wrapped, fringed skirt reaching to the knee. Women seem not to have achieved much recognition, for their portrayal is rare; their costume appears to have been very similar to that of the man.

For headgear, kings and priests wore cylindrical hats with horizontal or vertical fluting, and sometimes a tall fez with an inverted cone on top. Men of lesser importance wore a smaller fez or an ornament tied around their tightly curled or elaborately braided hair. Women liked to interlace beads with their natural hair, or sometimes they wore little crown-shaped hats.

Well-designed sandals, which covered the heels, were the fashionable footgear, although some warriors are shown wearing high, laced boots.

Figure 6. Reproduction from a bas-relief representing a scene of rite in which animals are brought to the sacrifice.

The long, squared beards and the elaborate stylization of their long hair testify to their fondness for ornamentation. Both men and women adorned themselves with huge earrings, heavy bracelets, armlets, tassels, and richly embroidered tunics.

THE PHOENICIANS

The Phoenicians, who settled along the eastern coast of the Mediterranean, assimilated Egyptian and Sumerian experience, adopting Mesopotamian techniques and traditions. Because of the long, narrow shape of their country, they directed their life primarily toward the sea and they became expert in navigation and commerce. The Phoenicians established many contacts with the rich merchants of the Nile (as can be seen in some paintings in Egyptian tombs of the New Kingdom), and they ventured far abroad into the Mediterranean.

With Phoenicia came one of the most brilliant achievements of the old cultures—the invention of an alphabetic writing. Already in the time of Sargon, experts in cuneiform writing instructed scribes in all the large and small cities in order to diffuse the Sumerian culture. By 1500 B.C., priests and merchants of Ugarit had chosen twenty-nine characters of cuneiform used by their Babylonian teachers, assigning to them a phonetic value. Then, in the south of Phoenicia in a city still unknown, there was created another alphabet for the purpose of writing on papyrus, which was introduced by the Egyptians at Byblos. For this alphabet twenty-two signs denoting consonants were chosen, which appear to have been derived from Egyptian hieroglyphs.

The Phoenician dress was somewhat different from that of the other peoples of the Near East, and we have only rare

Figure 7. *Anatomic realism is also evident in this figure of an Assyrian deity. His singular costume seems to resemble the typical* kitonet *of the Phoenicians, and the hat is very similar to their* sarmat. *Detail reproduced from a bas-relief in alabaster from Ninevah, the last great capital of the Assyrian kingdom, Seventh Century* B.C.

examples of their costume. We know, however, that they wore a particular skirt called the *kitonet;* it was twisted around the hips, reaching from the waist to the knee or the calf, leaving the trunk naked. They wore hats of different types; one, called the *sarmat,* was singularly shaped and seems to have been made to protect the ears from the wind (Figure 7).

Mesopotamia 9

In Phoenicia we see an unusual society sustained in large part by the merchant class, independent of the ruling class. And with the diffusion of the art of writing came the ethically important result that the class of scribes was no longer a special, privileged class. So we can say that the Phoenicians, in a certain sense, appear as pioneers of a democratic society.

THE PERSIANS

The Persians, together with the Medes, differed both in language and appearance from the other peoples of Mesopotamia; taller, fairer of skin, they were the first Aryan type to dominate the great valleys. Under Darius I (521–485 B.C.) was fashioned one of the greatest land empires of western history, a masterpiece of organization from a civil as well as a military point of view.

Great similarity of costume existed among all these peoples, but the Persians were more reserved in their way of life and this attitude was reflected in their dress, which covered them almost completely (Figures 8, 9). Both men and women wore long, bloused Oriental trousers, called *anaxiride,* which they tucked into soft shoes; over these they wore long cloaks, or knee-length belted tunics, all expertly tailored. The Persian men wore long beards, and they often wore a draped headgear, through the pleats of which only the face showed (Figure 10).

Figure 9. A rare example of the most typical Persian costume giving a precise indication of the draping of the headgear and of the long tunic. Detail of bas-relief from the Palace of Persepolis, Fifth Century B.C. Persepolis was the capital of the Achaemenians, great conquerors and the ruling dynasty of Persia's huge empire for over two hundred years. Louvre, Paris. (Below.)

History of Fashions

Originally all of these costumes were white or the natural color of the fibers used in the fabrics. Gradually, however, with the development of a sense of color and with the knowledge of new techniques, dresses were painted and embroidered with stripes, circles, disks, triangles, and rhombs, usually in blue and red. The decorative motifs from the dresses, or from the borders and frames of Assyrian–Babylonian pictures, make very interesting designs for modern fabrics. The stylized fabrics of their costumes give us a precise idea of their conception of decoration (Plate 2).

The ornament of fringe, common to many of these peoples, appears to have been derived from the wide use of animal skins for their earliest clothes. These were not sewed, but

Figure 10. Darius and Xerxes holding audience. This bas-relief from the apadana of the Palace of Persepolis shows the typically draped costume and squared beards of the Persians. Photo courtesy of the Oriental Institute, University of Chicago, Chicago, Illinois.

simply adjusted to the body to protect it from the cold; then later, the pelt was cut at the bottom of the fashioned garment to allow for more freedom of movement. The resulting fringe eventually became a decorative element of the costume.

Herodotus of Halicarnassus (484–406 B.C.), the famous historical writer of antiquity—justly called "the father of history"—has given us a marvelous picture of all this old, Oriental world; he wove, from the origins, the history of the people that composed it. Avidly desiring to know and to understand foreign peoples and regions, he traveled through Thessaly, Phoenicia, Egypt, and Babylonia. He visited Babylon one and a half centuries after it had become the most beautiful city of the old world under the reign of Nebuchadnezzar II. Thus he was able to describe the wonderful and original city that radiated the brilliance of this civilization, which flourished in Babylonia but drew from the contributions of all the surrounding peoples.

These populations participated in a continuous process of refinement of techniques and costumes, gradually losing their individual characteristics, so that when political unification was ripe, it confirmed and welded together all that which was more deeply common to all of them. Among the evident common heritages was the costume, which maintained the line of the Babylonia of Nebuchadnezzar throughout many centuries.

In all those countries the new economy exacted and created conventional systems of writing, accounting, weights and measures, and division of time, revolutionizing the methods of accumulating knowledge and transmitting experience. And naturally the new economy produced new sciences.

All these civilizations which originated and developed in Mesopotamia represent one of the most significant periods in history.

History of Fashions

Egypt

Ancient Egypt must be considered in the historic light of an extinct Oriental civilization. The desert and the cataracts of the Nile isolated it from the rest of Africa, and the region of the Nile flourished with a culture that we now know as one of the richest, greatest, and most elegant in history. It was a colossal civilization, enduring for many thousands of years from the most remote prehistory until about 1000 B.C., when its native rule fell before the invader. Egyptian history commonly is dated by the dynasties of its pharaohs, or by broader groupings of those dynasties known as the Old Kingdom, the Middle Kingdom, and the New Kingdom.

All that we know of the Egyptian people before the dynasties we deduce from their graves which preserved many of the original particulars of their way of life: vases for food and drink, gear for fishing and hunting, cosmetics and other articles for the toilette, precious and semiprecious stones, slate tablets, and so on. Successively, the inhabitants turned from hunting to fishing and agriculture—a fact affirmed by the many boats painted on their vases. Those same vases testify

Figure 11. Head of Chefren protected by the divine falcon. Diorite statue from the Temple of the Sphinx, Gizeh Fourth Dynasty. Cairo Museum.

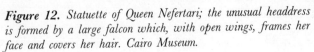

Figure 12. Statuette of Queen Nefertari; the unusual headdress is formed by a large falcon which, with open wings, frames her face and covers her hair. Cairo Museum.

to new techniques and chemicals used for the decoration of pottery. And at that time the art of porcelain making was introduced. But archaeological documentation reveals no evidence of kings; it was still a simple society, however specialized its artisans. Nor were there yet examples of writing; it was to appear later in the royal tombs with words written in ink on terra-cotta or wood, but not for many centuries on papyrus.

About 3000 B.C. the economical situation exacted the development of writing, the sciences, and the creation of the state. All the social and economic organizations in ancient Egypt, which evolved because of its special geographic location, appear to have been created by one called Menes—leader of the clan of the Falcon and himself identified as the Divine Falcon. This is explained in written records found in the royal tombs. And for centuries the falcon persisted as the symbol of divinity in a great many Egyptian paintings and sculptures (Figures 11, 12).

The evident contrast between the tombs of the rich and the poor, especially the wealth of the monumental tombs of the pharaohs, indicates not only the severe division of the social classes, but also the special significance attributed to the god-kings. The Egyptians believed that even after death the king must continue to exert his magic protection for the populace; and concentrated in the pharaonic tombs were all the treasures produced by the land and by man. The richest was the huge pyramid of Cheops which, according to Herodotus, required twenty years and 100,000 men to construct. One of the most fascinating tombs is that of the famous Queen Nefertari; it is full of magnificent frescoes which are singular for the delicate design and the splendor of the colors (Figure 13).

The recovery of the ancient world and its rich treasures was an indirect result of Napoleonic imperialism. When Napoleon conducted his military expedition into Egypt in 1798, he took

Figure 13. Nefertari, queen of Ramses II of the Nineteenth Dynasty, was deified after death to protect the Theban necropolis. Here she is wearing a white tunic with long stoles of contrasting green and red; the necklaces are in gold; and the skin of her face, hands and feet are painted in blue. Many rites of ancient Egypt required that the personage be painted in blue or in green. Fresco, British Museum, London.

with him many surveyors and engineers to explore the land and to make geographic drawings and maps; he also brought scholars to study the history. This handful of men prepared the famous "Description of Egypt" (1809–1813) for the Academy of France. And this was the beginning of the scientific study of that unknown civilization. After twenty years of work the philologist J. F. Champollion succeeded in deciphering the Egyptian alphabet from the famous Rosetta Stone (found by an officer of Napoleon) and thereby opened the way for recouping the lost world. This was one of the most significant events in the recording of history.

Al Kemia, meaning the black land, is the oldest name of Egypt, and from it derived the word alchemy, then chemistry; thus this modern science takes its name from the people who were the most proficient in that field in ancient times. Through the practice of embalming their dead, the Egyptians acquired a thorough knowledge of anatomy and established the beginnings of the science of medicine.

The arts of metallurgy and dyeing in Old Egypt gave rise to the first forms of organized labor and craftsmanship; industries were created in which huge numbers of slaves were occupied. Class differentiation developed on an extensive scale and out of it evolved a leisure and opulent class which could devote itself entirely to art and science, thereby playing a crucial part in the growth of civilization. An important result of Egyptian science was the creation of the solar calendar, from which our calendar derives, and which certainly was inspired by the recurrent flooding of the Nile in Egypt.

All that has been excavated and discovered provides us with a precise idea of Egyptian life and culture, which distinguished itself for progress in agriculture, science, social life, and handicrafts. In fact, we can see from the paintings that they constructed boats, loomed fabrics and carpets, and produced perfumes and jewels.

The fact that we know the Egyptians principally from their tombs leads us to ignore other qualities of their character, taste, and spirit. From some farcical stories about their deities, which seemed to amuse them so much, we know that they were gifted with joviality and a fine sense of humor, and an evident freedom of thought. They did not neglect public or private amusements; they played dice and chess, exercised themselves in games of swimming, boxing, and fighting with bulls (Figure 14). For their games and feasts, they liked to be annointed with perfumed oils by their servants, and they wore garlands of flowers and exchanged gifts.

Plato described the Athenians as lovers of knowledge, and the Egyptians as lovers of wealth. Really, they were in the old world much like the Americans are today, enamored of magnificence and beauty, dedicated to gigantic works of construction, and believing in a peace which they thought could be achieved through prosperity and refinement.

Figure 14. *This surprising fresco of a ball game is from the tomb of Beni Hasan, Twelfth Dynasty. The hairdressings are interesting and made up of thin braids and tassels. The players wear white, transparent* kalasyris *with simple, dark collars; bracelets adorn the wrists and ankles. Cairo Museum.*

Egypt

Figure 15. *Detail of a mural on stucco from the Theban tomb of Djeserkura of the Eighteenth Dynasty. The lady and her hand-maiden both wear the perfume cone on top of their remarkable hair-dos. The costume of the maid consists of a simple* cache-sexe *made of gold thread held with lapis lazuli. The designs of the lady's neck-lace and bracelets are very graceful as is the assymetrical decolletage of her* kalasyris. *Her chair, elegant in line, with legs shaped like a lion's, is the prototype of the "Empire Style." Cairo Museum.*

The importance they attributed to social life is evident in the care and grooming of their person and in their refined costume (Figure 15). Also, from the appearance of these hieratic figures, we can understand how important to them was the etiquette of public life. A sort of pleasing equilibrium emanates from all of this general care, which gives us an idea of the high level of this civilization.

In Egypt, as in most other ancient civilizations, there was no theater; the religious rite was the spectacle. Because of their belief in immortality, elaborate ceremonies were performed to prepare the dead for judgment by the gods who would determine the ultimate destination of the soul. Chief among their gods were Osiris and his sister-wife Isis, who were identified with the Nile and fertility, and later, Amon-Ra and Aton, the sun-gods. But there are many scenes of rites in which deities are masked with the heads or bodies of birds, goats, and other animals (Figure 16).

History of Fashions

Figure 16. *The goddess Amentit is seated near the god-king Harakhti. This is one of a series of frescoes which covered the walls of the tomb of Queen Nefertari. The frescoes are singular for their excellence of design and splendor of colors, making this one of the most beautiful and evocative tombs of Thebes. The goddess wears a wig with the infula, bracelets, armlets, and a tightly fitted* kalasyris *supported by a collar of beads. The god-king wears a mask symbolizing the divine falcon. Cairo Museum.*

Figure 17. These three fishermen pulling in the net show a very nice, scant costume; it is composed of just a cord knotted in front and falling like a brief pendant. Clearly visible is the net full of fish with corks holding it afloat. From the Staatliche Museum, Berlin.

Boats are nearly ever-present in Egyptian paintings; sometimes they express the obsessive preoccupation with a cult of death and the journey the soul had to make; other times they tell the story of a man's life and work (Figure 17). Often these slender boats indicate the departure of fishermen; and these are pictured with two birds: one for catching fish, and the other a falcon for luck. Still other boats are depicted in front of hunting scenes along the river, among beautiful waterlilies.

Many panels have been found which portray both black and white people. Sometimes this portrayal indicates the different races in Egypt, and sometimes the artists deliberately used the black figures to set off the white ones in order to give more spatial quality to the paintings, since they did not use perspective. In general, an earth-red color distinguished the flesh of men, ocher-yellow of women.

History of Fashions

The Egyptians were the first to have a literary form that we might consider as books. The "Book of the Dead" and the "Book of Breathings" are two of the most famous papyrii, dating from 3300 B.C. or earlier. The material was handed down for generations and many copies survive from the New Kingdom. Both of these books are essentially religious in nature, but we know that the Egyptians also had a delightful secular literature of love and fantastic adventure.

It appears that they were also dedicated to music, for there are many pictures of musicians with harps, and girls with unusual, fanciful instruments.

All the motifs that we find in Egyptian paintings can and do nourish our fantasy and put us nearer to that mysterious old world. Although they have a special significance for historians and archaeologists, the motifs can be useful in suggesting many ideas for the design of contemporary fabrics. Some vases in alabaster, for example, found in a corner of the entrance to the tomb of Tutankhamen, reveal an elegant profile and exquisite workmanship of the designs; after 3300 years, traces remain of the original perfume contained in them.

In one of the most famous tombs, that of Meket-re, were assembled many little statues, boats, and models of the life and occupations of the dead man. Famous is a girl wearing a painted or embroidered *kalasyris*, with jewels at her neck, wrists, and ankles. Her feet are bare, and on her head she carries a basket of fruits and vegetables (Figure 18). The

Figure 18. *A statuette found in the Eleventh Dynasty tomb of Meket-re is a typical example of the less formal Middle Kingdom sculpture. This maiden wears a colored* kalasyris *with an interesting design imitating peacock feathers; diagonal straps support the dress, and around the neck is the typical beaded collar. Louvre, Paris.*

Figure 19. Objects found in the tomb of Tutankhamen at Thebes reveal personal aspects of the young pharaoh's life. Cairo Museum.

statuette is of wood and the colors are very vivid. Another represents a servant carrying a cosmetic case, which appears extraordinarily modern.

We can see in the tomb of Tutankhamen particular hairdos, models of costumes, and the richest of all the decorative elements. The major part of his throne is completely covered with laminated gold leaf, inlaid with ceramic, colored glass, and stones of very fine cut. The back of the throne is a bas-relief showing the pharaoh in his palace, sitting with his wife; over them is the sun, radiating Life, which is symbolized by rays ending in little hands.

In the same tomb were found many objects of interest, such as weapons in terra-cotta and gold, boxes to hold game from hunting, interesting buckles for the royal sandal in gold and precious stones, and even some memories of the Tutankhamen childhood were found in a little coiffe of very fine linen, covered by golden disks. It is extraordinary to see, also, a little glove from so long ago! There were folding stools with hinges in gold, the seat rigid in ebony and ivory; some were covered with a fabric very modern in taste and design (Figure 19).

Egypt   23

Figure 20. *The mummy of Tutankhamen was found enclosed in three sar-cophagi. The outer one is of gilded, carved wood; the second is also in gilded wood but is encrusted with multicolored, crushed glass; the inner is of 22 carat gold, six feet long, and weighing about four hundred pounds. The large head of the first casket shows the details of the false beard and clearly indicates the character-istics of the stylized makeup which the Egyptians normally used. Cairo Museum.*

The statue of Tutankhamen at the entrance was carved in wood, made black with bitumen, and dressed magnificently in gold leaf. It is more than nine feet tall, and it gives us an idea of the fabulous wealth of the pharaohs. Tutankhamen wears a skirt with a rigid panel; on his head is the *klaft,* and on his forehead the *uraeus,* the sacred asp. The klaft is a particular Egyptian hat used by men, and also by women, of high class. It consisted of a piece of fine cloth, specially folded, and gen-erally striped in blue, green, and gold (Figure 20).

In the early dynasties, the dress of the Egyptians was ex-tremely simple: the men wore a loin cloth drawn between their

Figure 21. Menkure and his Queen, Fourth Dynasty. This important statue embodies the timeless dignity of Old Kingdom funerary sculpture. Menkure is shown wearing the most classic klaft, skent, and false beard; the queen wears a transparent kalasyris and a rigid, large wig. Courtesy Museum of Fine Arts, Boston.

Figure 22. Hunting and fishing scene from the Eighteenth Dynasty tomb of the scribe, Nakht. This little tomb in Thebes is particularly noted for its exceptional state of preservation and for its fresh and vivid murals. The central male figure wears the skent *and over it a transparent* pano. *The profile reveals the line of a false beard, and he wears a rich collar and bracelets. The painting is completed by two feminine figures and a little girl wearing a costume of only a string of pearls. It is singular to note that women and men both show their nails covered with mother-of-pearl enamel. Cairo Museum.*

legs and wrapped around the hips; then a short wrap-around skirt, called the *skent* (Figure 21). Women wore a long, tight kalasyris, reaching from under the breast to the ankle, held up by one or two shoulder straps, or a collar of various kinds of beads and bones.

Later, the male skirt lengthened to the knee, midcalf, or ankle and was worn with a specially knotted girdle. The kalasyris sometimes appeared pleated to allow more freedom for walking; the women achieved a sort of modern *plissé* by carefully pleating dampened fabric and placing it under the weight of heavy stones. By the Fifth Dynasty, the male skirt was designed with rigid triangular points in the front, or it was stiffened into a trapezoidal shape. During the Middle Kingdom, men wore varied types of skents, often placing over the loin-skirt a long overskirt of transparent material, called *pano* (Figure 22).

In the New Kingdom the kalasyris at times was worn by men as well as women. Skirts became more complex with combinations of overskirts, which often were tucked up and puffed out. Both men and women assumed full, transparent, and marvelously pleated kalasyres, which, when fastened in front of the breast, formed a sort of cape over the arms.

As in succeeding civilizations, dress in ancient Egypt was used as a symbol of rank. The pharaoh's skirt was of a special shape with rounded points, richly ornamented in gold. A royal apron, often suspended from the girdle, was elaborately decorated with colored leathers, golden beads, or glass in a stylized design of lions' heads and rows of asps.

The crown of Upper Egypt was a tall, white cone with a knob on top; that of Lower Egypt was red, shaped like a basket with a tall extension at the back. When the North and South Kingdoms were unified, the king wore a combination of the two crowns, known as the Pharaoh's Crown or *pschent*, adopting the name of Lower Egypt's Crown (Figure 23).

History of Fashions

Figure 23. *This triptych shows three elegant images: the first is a sovereign wearing the* pschent *of Lower Egypt; the second is the goddess Isis, as can be seen by the moon held in her lyre-shaped headdress; the third shows a king wearing the crown of Upper Egypt before the unification of the two kingdoms. Staatliche Museum, Berlin.*

Figure 24. *Painted bas-relief from the tomb of Prince Djehuty-hetep at El Bersheh, showing the daughter of the Prince, c. 1850* B.C. *Cairo Museum.*

The priest dressed in a simple white linen skirt (wool was considered impure and fit only for barbarians); for ceremonial occasions he donned the traditional leopard skin. The priest is always seen without a wig; his head, indeed his entire body, was clean-shaven as a symbol of purity.

On the banks of the Nile, the premarital costume of the girls was easy and free; and the dancers, who wore precious and diaphanous dresses, were much sought after in the ambience of high society.

The clothes in general were white, made of a special transparent fabric, very similar to the light batiste of linen (Figure 24). Color was used only in the most imaginative decorations made of real feathers or of painted designs, which imitated plumage or the hides of animals.

History of Fashions

The ornaments, on the contrary, were very colorful and were always created in primary hues of full intensity, because the Egyptians ignored the nuances, the subtle middle tones. The earliest ornaments, of course, were simple, made with a piece of colored fabric, or with animal and vegetable elements: leaves, flowers, bones, shells, and common stones found in the sand of the desert or on the beaches of the Nile. These came before the time of the real jewels made of precious metals and stones (Plate 3).

The Egyptian people had a vivid sense of decoration, and, being expert chemists, they dedicated themselves to the art of cosmetics, painting their faces, eyes, mouths, fingernails, and correcting the blemishes of nature. The adults adorned themselves with necklaces and pendants, and wore precious amulets in the center of the forehead. These usually represented a little serpent with the head of a vulture, which served to protect them from evil.

They had sandals made of woven papyrus and palm leaf, some with precious buckles and turned-up toes. Out of a fastidious regard for cleanliness, the Egyptian men were clean-shaven, but they were wont to display the badge of manly dignity by wearing artificial beards. These were small braided beards, the king's being longer than that of private citizens, and often turned up at the end. Sometimes ornate "beards" for both kings and queens were fashioned out of precious materials, even jewels, and attached to the chin.

Both men and women shaved their heads or clipped their hair short, and then they wore extraordinary wigs made from wool dyed blue, or monkey hair, and sometimes from vegetable fibers, elaborated with great fantasy. The splendor and size of the wig varied according to the importance of the person wearing it. The ladies loved sophisticated hairdressing; some diadems show a special cleverness and a particular re-

Egypt

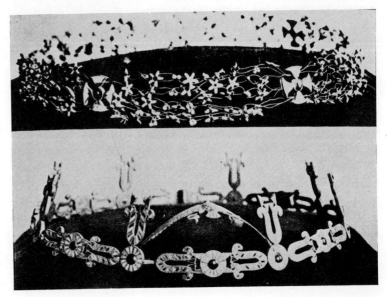

Figure 25. *Splendid examples of Egyptian diadems made in gold, silver, enamel, and precious stones: two of them are infulae, which were worn on the wig; the upper one is in silver and would seem to be a garland from the Renaissance time it is so extraordinarily delicate and well crafted. Museum of Leida, Holland; Cairo Museum.*

Figure 26. *A fragment from the famous bas-relief in rock, Tell-at-el-Amarna, depicts the adoration of the energy of the sun's rays. This cult became a national religion when Amenohotep IV assumed the name of Akhenaton, meaning the "splendor of Aton"—aton being the name for the sun. Cairo Museum; Art Reference Bureau.*

Figure 27. Nefertiti, queen of the Eighteenth Dynasty of Thebes, wife and sister of Akhenaton. This particular type of beauty was recreated c. 4000 years later in the paintings of Modigliani and remains the ideal feminine image of our time. Balenciaga, in 1953, imposed the image of Nefertiti on the fashion world, imitating her makeup and even her famous hat, and proved how it is possible to find new inspiration from ancient costumes. Egyptian Museum, Berlin.

finement, which were not to be equaled in delicate taste until the Eighteenth Century (Figure 25).

In contrast with the adult finery, the children went almost naked; just at the waistline they sometimes wore a string of pearls and lapis-lazuli intertwined. Princes of the royal house at times wore a multibraided lock of hair or decorations symbolizing the young god Horus; this was often a falcon with its large wings spread across the chest.

The Egyptian woman seems to have been an affectionate mother and a devoted companion to her husband. Many tomb paintings and reliefs, some of high ceremonial nature, indicate that the Egyptian woman, in comparison to women of other old societies, had a position of liberty and equality with the men. More important in the society of the time was the place given by caste rather than the difference in sex (Figure 26).

Nefertiti, Queen of the Eighteenth Dynasty of Thebes, of possible foreign origin to judge from the patrician, Euro–Asiatic profile, was the sister-wife of Ahkenaton. One famous sculpture of her head is conserved in the Museum of Berlin; it is among those sculptures that came from the ancient laboratory of Thutmes, where a notable series of masks in plaster were pressed from the faces of living models, or cadavers. The name Nefertiti signifies, "The most beautiful has arrived!"; and really, it is a perfect beauty, intellectually animated, which was the ideal type of Egyptian woman, and which, strangely, remains the ideal modern woman (Figure 27).

The society and life of Egypt were expressed in elevated customs, and in refined and elegant clothing. It was a civilization that endured longer than any other, and yet still speaks to the modern world through its three symbols: the pyramids, the Sphinx, and the Phoenix; the foundations of intellectual principles, religion, and philosophy.

Palestine

Palestine is the old Promised Land, so-called because it was the chosen fatherland of the Jews. Of all the peoples of earliest history, only one survives today to bring us closer to that mysterious world of the ancient Near Orient. The history of this people had a special destiny, as events have proved.

In the beginning, the Jews were a mixture of many races, deriving from crossed ethnic currents of the Near East and from more distant and less-known sources. But their type emerged with a remarkable constancy; they always had a special physical aspect and a fineness and obstinacy of spirit. When they emerged on the stage of history, they were nomadic Bedouins who feared the deities of the air and who worshipped the sun, rocks, bovines, and the spirits of the caverns and the hills (Figure 28).

By the time they entered Palestine and established an independent state, around 1400–1200 B.C., a strong monotheism had developed. Moses is believed to have married a Kenite girl, whose tribal god was Jaweh; under Moses, to whom he revealed the Ten Commandments, Jaweh became the supreme

Figure 28. A stele in limestone from the Fourteenth Century B.C. representing the fearsome god, Baal, with his terrible thunderbolt. Louvre, Paris.

tribal god of the Hebrews, Jehovah of the Old Testament. Moses never completely succeeded in dissuading the early Jews from adoration of the golden calf because Egyptian idolatry of the bull was still fresh in their memory; in fact, for a long time the symbol of Jaweh was the bovine.

That intense and somber religion never adopted some of the fine rites and joyous ceremonies that characterized the faith of the Egyptians and the Babylonians. The sentiment of the nonentity of man before his god made all of the ancient Jews' thoughts pessimistic. Religions of hope and love are born in security and order, but the necessity to impress the conquered and rebellious populace made the primitive religions faiths of mystery and fear.

In the period just before and after the fall of Jerusalem, 586 B.C., the prophets strengthened and purified the religion of the Jews and prepared them for an influential role in the Occidental World which later would be so affected by Christianity.

They were not one unified nation, but remained almost always divided into twelve tribes. They were organized not on the principles of a state, but on the principles of a patriarchal family, which was the source of their fascinating unity and strength.

Their language, similar to that of the Phoenicians, was beautiful and sonorous, and with it they created the finest literature of the ancient Orient.

Once settled in Palestine, the Hebrews became farmers and herdsmen, but in Solomon's reign they became important in the inland caravan trade; and they also developed a merchant fleet. In the old Orient, as today, the merchants not only traveled but also needed permanent offices and agencies in foreign cities. So in every port and capital there were traders, and everywhere the Jews were present.

For a very long time, the Hebraic Law had to combat idolatry and, for that reason, prohibited the representation of animals and persons. Therefore we have very few testimonies of the Hebrew costume; the examples we do have come to us through their contacts with other peoples, such as the Egyptians. In various Egyptian tombs, for example, bas-reliefs and frescoes were found which present some particulars of their dress. In the four centuries they were in Egypt, 1650–1220 B.C. according to the Bible, they assimilated the Egyptian costume and left behind many vestiges of their own. Their costume was very simple, but it had a great dignity and an austere character which we can interpret as a noble expression of survival of an oppressed people.

Like all the people of antiquity, the Jews wore a simple tunic with long sleeves folded back; but singular in their clothing were their own special types of overdresses. First, the *kaftan* (which they wore almost constantly since it was used for traveling); it was somewhere between a coat and a cloak, opened in front, reaching to the calf, and generally in the dark colors which the Jews normally preferred. The kaftan was sometimes held in at the waistline by a cord or various other belts, or often worn without a belt. They wore soft, large turbans or a sort of cowl in wool, very long behind and ending in a tassel.

Tassels also were placed in the corners of the *ephod*, a second typical overdress of their costume. The ephod was made of two rectangular pieces of fabric, sewed together at the shoulders, or of one very long rectangular piece with a hole in the center for putting the head through, opened at the sides like a poncho. Before long, the ephod became a religious dress and then it was decorated with amaranth-colored tassels.

Very early in their civilization, the Jews learned the art of weaving; in fact, their tunics are characteristic in that they were without seams, just woven on the loom. Their clothing was generally of wool, and sometimes of linen, but the two fabrics were never woven together because Hebraic Law prohibited the mixture of different fibers.

The high priests wore a special costume with three different types of tunics. Over the tunics they placed a little, short ephod, blue and red, which was held at the waistline by a golden cord. On the breast, they wore a very large and special jewel; it was square and composed of twelve different precious stones, representing the twelve tribes of Israel.

The Hebraic women were beautiful, and they enjoyed pleasing others. They liked elegant hairdressings, composed with pearls, and they used many perfumes and cosmetics. The women wore simple, but finely colored costumes; in general, over the pure white tunic with very wide, fan-shaped sleeves, they put a slender, long ephod, fastened at the hips by little gold clasps. The ephod was usually dark red; over it, they draped a very large cloak in different tones of red, sometimes ending at the two corners with gold-colored tassels of silk. The tassels had a special spherical form. The women were very clever at embroidering their dresses and fabrics for the house. Their embroidery was Oriental in taste; it was not simple, like their costume, but more elaborate, rich, and fine, like their aspirations.

The Jewish people wore their hair in the natural state, without wigs; and the men almost always wore a beard. The women left their hair long, falling on the shoulders, or arranged like a diadem around the forehead.

When someone died, women and men of the tribe expressed their grief by rending their clothing and going barefoot. Usually, however, they wore sandals.

In the schools of Palestine, the scribes and the rabbis composed a body of laws and comments, known as the Talmud, which became the holy law for the Jews. It is difficult to understand the Talmud in historic terms, because it was both the law and the history of survival of a humiliated people, oppressed and many times in danger of disintegration. The Talmud is composed, in fact, of wise advice, deep psychological insights, some majestic expressions of the Old Testament, and some tender expressions of the New Testament. It helped to quiet the troubled nature of the Hebrews, control their individualism, and make them sober and faithful before family and community; in short, it regulated their lives. So, after the fall of Jerusalem, the Jews had a law, but not a state; a book, but not a fatherland.

It is extraordinary that these people, so deprived but so civilized, and so tried by griefs, were able to conserve their dignity, austerity, and costume; and, above all, a great moral strength for survival.

The Prehellenic Period

For two thousand years, until about 1100 B.C., there existed a fascinating world which has come to be known as the Aegean civilization. Although the earliest culture and, consequently, the greatest refinements developed on the island of Crete, the civilization was spread throughout the many islands dotting the Aegean Sea, the western coast of Asia Minor, and the European peninsula we now know as Greece.

> It is a ground called Crete, which is in the middle of a dark sea, dark as wine, and it is a beautiful and rich ground, surrounded by waters . . . .

So wrote Homer. And, in fact, it was this large fertile island that produced one of the most artistic civilizations in history. Although its geographic location in the eastern Mediterranean—within sailing distance of Asia, Africa, and Europe—made the island a natural link for trade and commerce among other ancient civilizations, the Cretans preserved a unique and personal style.

Sir Arthur Evans, who began excavations at Knossos in 1900, uncovered this highly original and long-lasting civilization and named it Minoan, after the legendary King Minos. Indeed, he believed the Palace of Knossos, with its labyrinth of rooms and courtyards, to be the very building that inspired the story of Ariadne and Theseus, and the very fearsome Minotaur. The refinements of this palace, and those at Phaistos and Gournia, reveal that these peace-loving and maritime people also were ingenious architects and engineers: broad stairways, light wells, theaters, storerooms, and royal chambers make up the many-storied, intricate design. The palaces and the homes of the wealthy were equipped with an efficient plumbing system which was not to be equaled until Greek and Roman times.

Sir Arthur Evans originally had gone to Crete to discover the origins of a mysterious hieroglyphic writing found on tiny seal stones among the excavations at Mycenae, on the Peloponnesus. Surpassing his fondest dreams, hundreds of tablets eventually were uncovered, and he was able to identify two kinds of script.

There was ample evidence that this civilization knew the art of writing about 2000 years before Christ. For their business affairs the Minoans used a kind of pictographic writing—like the remains of the most ancient Sumerian writing. That which remains of ancient Cretan writing is almost exclusively inscribed on clay tablets, which remained a mystery until a short time ago. Only in 1956, when Michael Ventris decodified the so-called Linear B, was the enigma partially clarified; it appeared to be an archaic form of Greek, written with syllables and probably derived from an older Minoan writing. Sadly for scholars and romanticists, no literature has been discovered; the clay tablets either record grain rations, inventory prosaic items, or describe offerings to the gods. It seems incredible that this refined and imaginative people, in contact with Egypt and Mesopotamia, did not leave a comparable written literature.

Fortunately, the artist played an important role in the culture of Crete, hence we have many vivid pictures of a people devoted to gay and luxurious living. The palaces of Crete were lavishly decorated with frescoes painted in brilliant colors, depicting scenes of religious rites, lithe young men and women gathering flowers or engaged in acrobatic games, dolphins at play, and many decorative elements from nature.

The forms and the designs on their vases are audacious and full of young grace and spirit, qualities that characterize the Cretan style. The pottery is marvelous not only for the designs, but also for the variety: some pieces for storing olive oil are heavy, and tall as a man; others are so thin and delicate that they resemble the finest porcelain. These small "egg-shell" vases, coming from about 2100 B.C., were gaily decorated. Around 1500 B.C., fine vases appeared, designed with remarkable floral and marine forms in a lustrous black glaze. These vases certainly influenced the later Greeks, who, in fact, were indebted to Crete for the invention of the potter's wheel.

Some of the large jars were used as tombs, into which games and amusements for the dead person were placed. Sometimes a clay, or beautifully carved stone, "bathtub" was used as a coffin. The Cretans had a pleasant cult of the dead, putting into these strange tombs everything for the toilette, some things to eat, and even some figurines of attractive girls to keep the dead man company.

The Cretans had a varied theology comprising many different deities: the sun, the moon, goats, serpents, doves, and so on, and they imagined a sylvan population of nymphs and sileni. Priestesses were all-important, but on certain occasions men also took part in the celebration of cult rites.

The Prehellenic Period   **41**

Figure 29. *One of many terra-cotta statuettes representing the famous "Serpent Priestess." This surprising costume is composed of a skirt in volants and a fitted bodice with sleeves; the bodice is closed at the neck by a metal circlet but it is cut and wired to expose the breasts. The slender waist is marked by a corset-like belt with rolled borders, and a short apron with embroidered designs decorates the front of the skirt. Bracelets in the shape of serpents constrict the wrists, and on the large crown an owl sits, symbolizing protection. Marburg-Art Reference Bureau.*

Figure 30. *Jewel in gold designed with two bees; a pendant that belonged to Malia, Prince of Knossos, shows the granulation technique of goldworking. Candia Museum.*

Typical of Cretan sculpture, which was more decorative than monumental, are the statuettes in ivory, ivory and gold, and glazed terra-cotta. Famous is the "Goddess of Serpents," of whom many similar images were made (Figure 29). The originality of the design is very interesting, and indeed surprising if we think of the very remote period—about 5000 years ago. In this skirt, the volants resemble the *falbalas,* which will appear for the first time in the last years of the Seventeenth Century.

In metal work, also, the Cretans were superb craftsmen. In repoussé they created lovely floral patterns on gold cups and bronze vases, and they decorated bronze daggers with lively hunting scenes in gold and silver. This work was much admired and widely exported throughout the Aegean world (Figure 30).

It was an aristocratic civilization which left everything fine in art and in the costume. Cretan women were very feminine and dedicated to the gentle arts of weaving, embroidery, and the braiding of straw for baskets; but they also helped the men in the fields and in the pottery works. They appear to have enjoyed a position of respect and equality similar to their contemporaries in Egypt.

The feminine costume, so sophisticated and gay, was unlike any discovered in the ancient world, and it so astonished the French scholars of 1900 that they could compare the Cretan ladies only with the most fashionable ladies of their own times (Figure 31). The fully developed style, as seen in the statuettes, is composed of a cone-shaped skirt which seems to be held out by some wired undersupport, or underskirts; the tiny waist is constricted by a special belt, ridged and decorated; the unusual bodice laces above the waist and is cleverly contoured to support and, at the same time, expose the breasts; the sleeves are elbow-length and snugly fitted. Also very interest-

Figure 31. *Design from a statuette in painted clay (c. 1450* B.C.*) found in the excavations of Palaikastro on the island of Crete. The conical hat and the deep décolletage revealing the breasts are typical of the Cretan costume.*

Figure 32. From the famous restored fresco, "The Ladies in Blue," found in the Palace of Knossos and conserved in the Candia Museum. The elaborate and sophisticated hairdressing is notable.

ing are the motifs of the basque and apron on the skirt; they, too, will appear in the Seventeenth and Eighteenth Centuries, a time when the maturity of taste in the costume will be fullgrown. The elements of this ancient costume will continue to be used until the modern epoch; and still, today, we find the motifs of the bodice and skirts in native country costumes.

The "Ladies in Blue" (Figure 32), a famous fresco from Knossos, so very well restored, shows especially well the typical feminine hairdo of long curls, interlaced with pearls; the men's hair was arranged in almost the same way. Common was the style of these long curls escaping from a ribbon or band encircling the head: the classic *spira*, which we will see revived for use in the Greek and Roman theater.

The Cretan women, beautiful and elegant, assisted in the theater and took part in the games. One painting shows court ladies, with some important-looking men, observing the spectacles. In their gaily colored dresses, sitting with their legs tucked under them and gossiping in friendly attitudes, they seem to belong to a contemporary scene. We know of their theaters from the ruins found at Phaestos and Knossos, but unfortunately no literature of the theater has come to light. Perhaps they had only performances of dance and games.

The "Prince of Lilies" (Figure 33) one of the many stuccos decorating the Knossos Palace, represents a young man wearing a crown made of lilies and peacock feathers; a lily motif also creates the chain necklace he wears. His short skirt, horseshoe-shaped and dipping down in back, was probably cut to allow more freedom in walking. This abbreviated skirt is very small in the waistline, but the profile is thickened with a special belt, molded like a little corset; the belt has a rolled border in relief, which was a typical part of both the feminine and masculine costumes.

A wraparound loin skirt, again with the tight waist girdle, was another garment worn by men. This was richly patterned with a decorative border, ending in front with a pendant, beaded tassel.

Often in the paintings we see attractive dancing girls carrying jars or musical instruments which seem to accompany the steps of a dance. Sometimes they are wearing divided skirts trimmed with geometric decorations, appliquéd and alternated in colors. Other times the skirts are overlapped and trimmed with narrow, colored tapes. Ribbons always retain the natural hair which falls in curls; and always the girls and the ephebic men appear smiling, as though they are leading a carefree life, animated by dances, plays, games, and music. This seems to be the expression of their civilization, so devoted to the arts, but in the sense of enjoying and playing with them more than with the idea of creating "pure" art. Their culture, then, so refined and intimate, seems to be more similar to the Oriental cultures than to all that we know as the classic Greek culture.

Figure 33. "The Prince of Lilies," beautiful fresco from Knossos where the common motif of lilies is repeated in the background, in the delicate necklace, and in the crown—even the butterfly is stylized in the same manner. Candia Museum.

The Prehellenic Period   45

MYCENAE AND TROY

The discovery of Troy and Mycenae by a Nineteenth-Century German, Heinrich Schliemann, would seem to be the material for a romantic novel: a poverty-stricken youth mastered twenty-two languages, amassed a huge fortune, and undertook at his own expense the excavation of an unpromising-looking hill in Asia Minor, all because he was convinced that Homer's great poems, the "Iliad" and the "Odyssey," were based on historical fact and not poetic invention. Scholars scoffed, but in 1871 Schliemann *did* uncover the site of Troy and a great treasure of jewels, which he believed had belonged to the beautiful Helen. That successive excavations proved his Troy to be a later city built on the ruins of the Homeric Troy does not detract from the importance of his amazing, intuitive find. Again, in 1876, his faith in Homer led him to the discovery of the grave shafts and buried, golden treasures of Mycenae on the Peloponnesus of Greece.

The feminine Mycenaean costume, as seen in frescoes appears to have been very similar to that of the Cretan ladies (Figure 34). Long, loose curls of hair escape from a diadem of lilies; the bodice is fitted, but open in front to reveal the bosom; and the divided skirt is trimmed with many bands of colored decorations.

The warriors and hunters of Mycenae, however, dressed very differently from the peaceful Minoans (Figure 35). They wore tunics that reached to mid-thigh, long hose, and ankle-high boots; their helmets apparently were made of leather and decorated with horns or boars' teeth. From paintings we can deduce that the Homeric heroes often defended their bodies with just the shield and the helmet (Figure 36). But Homer describes some military costumes with shining cuirasses, very similar to those of the later Greeks. We can see this style, for example, in a painted plate coming from Kameiros

Figure 34. "Lady with Casket," well-known fresco from Tiryns, a site near Mycenae. This image shows a line of costume very similar to the Cretan style. Long, serpentine curls fall on the ample bosom, while the hair over the forehead is shorter and curled to form a diadem. Like the Cretan ladies, she is wearing a divided skirt with horizontal bands of decoration. National Archaeological Museum, Athens.

Figure 35. *Warrior Vase from Mycenae. Details of the leather helmet, both protected and adorned with boars' tusks as described by Homer, can be seen clearly. National Archaeological Museum, Athens.*

Figure 36. *This scene from a red-figure vase represents a duel between Hector and Achilles. Their armor consists of round shields and crested helmets. From Cerveteri.*

The Prehellenic Period

47

Figure 37. A painted plate from Kameiros, Rhodes, shows a duel between Menelaus and Hector. The decorations on the shields appear sophisticated for this early period. An obvious Oriental influence can be seen in the geometric and curvilinear ornamentation; in fact, the entire plate is covered with designs full of fantasy which can be used as a source for many contemporary decorations; c. Seventh Century B.C.

Figure 38. This interesting engraving validly describes a theatrical costume for the goddess Athena/Minerva. The tunic is particularly stylized and linear—appropriate, then, for the theater. Author's collection.

Figure 39. *Interesting necklace made of gold pendants decorated with rampant lions and stylized images of deities with wings. British Museum, London.*

(Figure 37) which shows Hector and Menelaus fighting near the fallen body of Euphorbus: the tunics are brief, but the decorated shields are very important. Homer also mentions huge shields ". . . like a tower, made of bronze and seven layers of leather. . . ." References to those body shields puzzled scholars, who had never seen anything like them until their depictions in frescoes and on seals and daggers were uncovered in the excavations at Mycenae and later at Knossos.

We can only speculate as to how the Trojan citizen dressed, for no great tombs with preserved remains have been uncovered; apparently cremation was practiced for centuries, and only ash and bones were placed in funeral jars. Also, great

The Prehellenic Period

fires destroyed the successive cities, so that no frescoes remain to tell the story. But bone or clay loom weights and spindles were found in the ruins, attesting to the fact that cloth was woven; and, from the numbers of sheep bones found, it must have been wool. Although Helen of Troy had precious, refined jewels, she probably wore tunics and cloaks of primitive design. In contrast to the extraordinarily modern and coquettish Cretan costume, the Homeric dress was almost rudimentary, a prelude to the classic Greek line.

When we prepare spectacles for the theater which concern Homeric tragedies, we generally use an archaic costume, stylizing the characters and the deities according to their traditional roles. Thus Athena, for example, will be dressed with a long, linear tunic and a brief silver cuirass with scales; a high crest and lance complete the typical costume of the warrior-goddess. In reality, we adopt a costume corresponding to the descriptions of Homer (Figure 38).

The art of goldworking must be considered exceptional in the Prehellenic civilizations if we consider the chains, collars, bracelets, and diadems, made generally of little gold medals and fringes; brooches adorned with animals, flowers in gold, beads in crystal and quartz; rings in spirals made of gold and silver filigree, pendants and earrings; rings with carnelian, amethyst, and agate stones; and for men, large rings with scenes of war engraved on the stones (Figure 39).

Looking at all this wealth of jewels, emblems, and symbols, it was possible for Schliemann to reconstruct and relive all the famous events and legends of the royal personalities: Agamemnon, the heroic old Hecuba, the sweet Andromache—widow of Hector, and the priestess, Cassandra, prophesying dire catastrophes. We can see from Schliemann's marvelous adventure how history and legend combine—and a dream becomes reality.

Greece

The contact with five cultures—Cretan, Mycenaean, Achaean, Dorian, Oriental; the immigrations and invasions that flowed into Greece, especially the Dorian and the Achaean; the wars of fortune—all these factors concurred to produce a mixture of races which, through the centuries, created the new Greek civilization.

The wars and invasions had destroyed all the marvelous bases of the great Minoan civilization and created a new world with a new spirit. By 800 B.C. the Greeks had lost all direct contact with their old world—probably only dim memories of former glories survived in the form of legends, for even the art of writing had been lost. But, as their position in the traffic and commerce of the Mediterranean became strong, they absorbed and adopted some themes and techniques from other peoples.

And the costume, with no extant examples of the amazing Cretan and Mycenaean achievements, was reborn with absolutely simple and primitive forms (Figure 40). For centuries the most harmonious and pure seminudity prevailed—not

Figure 40. Archaic statue of a virgin (Kore) in a very simple dress. Typical of this period is the hairstyle composed of long braids which leave the ears uncovered. Acropolis Museum, Athens; Marburg-Art Reference Bureau.

51

Figure 41. Beautiful archaic sculpture from Samos represents Hera and displays the purest Ionic form of Greek elegance. Louvre, Paris; Alinari-Art Reference Bureau.

because of neglect of the costume, but as an expression of the new philosophy which professed a substantial confidence in nature and in man, educating both his body and spirit.

Greek art reflects this concept of man and the special world of Greek civilization. Greek religious and philosophical thought elaborated this world into extraordinarily evolved forms which have remained as the foundations of the civilized and artistic riches of humanity to this day.

Perhaps we can say that Europe was born in the Greek civilization, because the Greeks certainly diffused this concept of man, a new philosophy, and the humanistic spirit that later bound together all European populations and was commonly called the "European Spirit."

The philosophic tendency, though deeply Occidental, nevertheless was linked to some precious Oriental heritage. We find the Oriental influence in Greece in vase paintings, bas-reliefs, and sculptures showing an archaic frontality and rigorous symmetry, which apparently were derived from the Egyptian school (Figure 41).

From beginning to end, Greek painting remained an art of line and silhouette; painted vases and frescoes were the forms of expression preferred by Greek painters. The beautiful vases describe the Greek costume in detail, and many of them have an exceptional artistic value. Delightful designs on vases, full of movement and grace, report to us even some games and light pleasures. For example, from one charming design we can see that girls in old Greece loved to play on a swing (Figure 42).

The Greeks had such a large vase trade that it is possible to find them everywhere in Europe, and especially in southern Italy where some of the most important and beautiful specimens have been found. In excavated tombs some excellent Attic black-figure *Kylix* were uncovered, showing banquet

Figure 42. *A drawing from a vase painting shows a game of swinging. Evident in both of these costumes is the* chlaina, *a sort of overskirt draped around the hips that Greek women used especially while working. The standing girl wears a special coiffe in linen, called* sacea, *and the Ionic chiton.*

Greece

scenes enlivened by singing and dancing maenads and musicians (Figure 43). Maenads were bacchants, that is, inebriated "possessed" women, performing at feasts in Bacchus' honor. Dancing furiously, crowned with grape leaves and ivy, they usually held the *thirsus,* a pole made of intertwined bunches of ivy, heather, and grape leaves (Figures 44a and b).

Since the time of the Renaissance, collections of gold and antique jewels were started which now constitute the main core of several modern museums. Even Pliny the Elder mentions such collections, called *dactyliothecae,* treasured by Hellenistic rulers and wealthy Roman art patrons. But despite this extremely diffused knowledge of old gold ornaments, only in the last decades has antique jewelry been studied scientifically.

Figure 44. *Paintings from the so-called Cup of Oltos. Of remarkable size and beauty, this cup is attributed to the great Attic painter, Oltos, who was active near the end of the Sixth Century* B.C. *(a) One of a group of Nereides wearing an original chiton decorated with small animals and serpents. (b) From the central group on the cup, Heracles, clad in a lion's skin, is represented grappling with Nereus and shows a very interesting hairdo. Villa Giulia, Rome.*

a

b

Figure 46. *A pair of splendid g bracelets in the form of a human cou, with the bodies of serpents. Third C tury* B.C.; *Metropolitan Museum, N York; Rogers fund 1956.*

Figure 45. *Pendant earring with beautiful filigree work in the form of rosettes, palmettes, and other abstract designs from plant life. Fourth Century* B.C. *National Archaeological Museum, Taranto.*

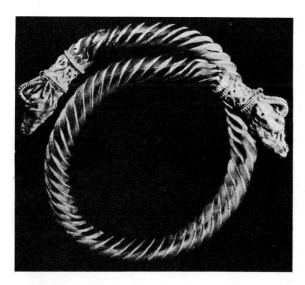

Figure 47. A bracelet of twisted gold with terminal decorations in the form of rams' heads. National Archaeological Museum, Taranto.

More than many other archaeological finds, antique jewelry is frequently impossible to date precisely. The difficulty arises from the repetition of some types produced through the centuries with identical motifs, and also by the transmission of heirlooms from generation to generation. Even today it is disputed whether some archaic jewels came from the laboratories of Magna Graecia or Etruria. One of the most famous arguments involves the precious necklace of Ruvo from the end of the Sixth Century B.C., now conserved at the archaeological National Museum of Naples.

A pair of earrings of the Fourth Century B.C., presently at the National Archaeological Museum of Taranto, surely can be attributed to the classic art of Magna Graecia (Figure 45).

Almost all bracelets were designed in a serpent shape and chiseled in gold. Some of these serpent-shaped bracelets look as if they were made by Benvenuto Cellini and, certainly, they must have inspired him (Figures 46, 47).

Figure 48. *Fine, delicate work appears in this gold and enamel diadem from Canosa. National Archaeological Museum, Taranto.*

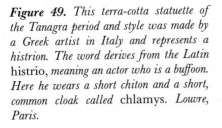

Figure 49. *This terra-cotta statuette of the Tanagra period and style was made by a Greek artist in Italy and represents a histrion. The word derives from the Latin* histrio, *meaning an actor who is a buffoon. Here he wears a short chiton and a short, common cloak called* chlamys. *Louvre, Paris.*

Figure 50. Hellenistic relief decorating a well. It shows the light weight chiton, softly draped with a hidden belt. National Museum, Rome.

The floral inspiration of diadems evidently derived from the flower crowns with which the young girls of antiquity adorned themselves (Figure 48).

The end of the Fourth Century B.C. brought the beginning of the decline of great Greek art. For about three centuries thereafter, a vivid artistic production flourished, but great artistic personalities seldom emerged. It was a period of exaggeration and imitation of classic art, but pure and sublime Greek art was to appear no more. We have, however, bas-reliefs and figures which give us faithful copies of the costume and show us that great care was devoted to it. Gracious and coquettish figures are portrayed in the well-known statuettes of Tanagra, which reflect the refinement of a rich artistic experience, but remain the expert work of artisans who were rich only in the possibilities and knowledge of technique (Figure 49).

The design of the Greek costume always consisted in the art of *drapery* and in the natural movement that the draped fabrics acquired according to the physical attitude of people wearing them (Figure 50).

The classic tunic, both for men and women, was called the *chiton*. It was one piece of fabric, in wool or linen, generally white, and gathered on the shoulders by clasps and cameos (Figure 51). The clasps, in general, were engraved with dance scenes for women and war scenes for men. In the Doric period the garment was made of wool which fell in heavy, natural folds; in later periods much lighter fabrics of linen were used, leading to a fantastic play of pleats, colors, and decorations (Figures 52, 53). The masculine chiton was usually short, with a hidden belt. Women likewise used hidden belts or cords, which determined soft blousing effects; and sometimes, with two belts, they wore the tunics twice-puffed.

Over the tunic they very often wore the famous peplum, a long rectangle of cloth fixed on both shoulders and falling along one hip in a special movement of folds, called *apoptygma* (Figure 54). Sometimes, the peplum was made from the top part of the chiton folded over.

Greek women wore their natural hair graciously arranged in varied hair styles, gathered on the back of the head by ribbons; the youngest sometimes tied their hair in a knot (Figure 55). Generally, they liked to decorate the hair with diadems, either of precious gold or plain leather, in the form of a half moon.

Figure 51. Athena with helmet and spear resting at a boundary stone. Her chiton with belt is typical of the Doric type: made in one piece which is folded over at the neck, it is held on the shoulders with clasps and tied at the waist with a cord. The wide pleats indicate a heavy material. Acropolis Museum, Athens.

Figure 52. A reproduction from a red-figure hydria shows two ladies spinning; they wear elegantly draped chitons of light, embroidered voile. Beads around their necks echo the design on their dresses.

Figure 53. *Athena with her special cuirass and helmet. From a black-figure vase describing a Panathenaic procession. Villa Giulia, Rome. (Left.)*

Figure 54. *Sacred dancers, from the metope of the Temple of Paestum, wear long tunics with the peplum falling along the hip into the* apoptygma. *(Below left.)*

Figure 55. *Artemis, the goddess of the moon and everlasting youth. Her charming hairdress is made from a knot of the natural hair. Third Century B.C. Louvre, Paris. (Below.)*

Greece

61

Figure 56. *A mosaic describing a scene in the grove of Academos where Plato taught. The philosophers are seen wearing the himation. National Museum, Naples.*

Figure 57. *Detail of an archaic sculpture shows the highly stylized hairdo of a young man. Louvre, Paris.*

Figure 58. *Bronze bust of Plato who lived from 428 to 327 B.C. The leather band around the head is typical of that age; often, the men used to tuck their longer hair up under the band. National Museum, Naples.*

Figure 59. *The famous "Charioteer of Delphi." A band in gold with the Greek key design encircles the head, and in his hands are the reins of the chariot. The sleeves of this tunic are particularly interesting and suggest solutions for contemporary costume. The wide, pleated tunic is held on the shoulder by slender cords. Delphi Museum; Alinari-Art Reference Bureau.*

The Greek cloak, a long, wide, draped rectangle, was called the *himation* and was commonly used by both sexes. It usually had a border trimmed with special designs, which, from the Hellenes, we call "Greek key" designs.

Philosophers wore the himation on the naked body, leaving one arm free for the gestures with which they liked to accompany their discourses (Figure 56).

The philosophers who followed Plato's doctrines expounded them in the house and in the large garden of the *Academos,* where Plato himself taught. From Academos came the word academy, which defines a school or university, that is, a sort of corporation of intellectual people, established with special regulations by public authority or private consensus, to cultivate the letters, sciences, or arts.

Women wore the himation over the tunic and draped it so that sometimes it even covered the head, in place of a hat. When traveling they often wore the Thessalic hat in straw, cone-shaped, and set on top of the cloak.

Men, too, very often wore diadems, always simpler and differently shaped from those of women, and at times as simple as a band tied around the forehead (Figures 57, 58). The male tunics also were varied in the movement or design of the pleats; sometimes they formed a sort of sleeve, particularly interesting in execution (Figure 59).

Greece   **63**

The military costume consisted of a very short tunic and a cuirass in metal with some engraved decorations on the breast and on the shoulders (Figure 60). Placed over the tunic was a very short skirt, made of strips of leather, to protect the body. The legs were protected from the knee down to the ankles by greaves in leather or in metal. Over the cuirass they sometimes wore a short cloak called the *chlamys*, fastened on the shoulders (Figure 61). The helmet was of varied shapes, with or without a visor.

In the early days, and for a long period of time, the Greeks went barefoot; later they began to wear sandals (Figure 62). Sandals with high cork soles were worn by some kings and, generally, by actors on the stage. Also deity figures were dressed with these *buskins*, since they increased the height and thereby the importance of the wearer.

With the great Greek civilization was born dramatic art: the first theater, the first theatrical costume. This was not really a theatrical costume, for actors wore the common dress, but, in order to have a special aspect on the stage, they sought the help of the buskins and created masks. Masks had the double function of characterizing the human types that they wanted to represent and amplifying the voice.

The invention of tragedy is attributed to Thespes, Greek writer of tragedies of the Sixth Century B.C. His story is legend: with his famous "traveling theater" he created the "introduction," given by the actor, and the "prologue." And he earned great success in the society of peripatetic philosophers, who had a tendency to organize the development of every literary subject.

The actors of Thespian tragedies used masks of linen and a special makeup; and they wore vine leaves in their hair. After Cherilo had elaborated the masks, Frinico, a pupil of Thespes, introduced feminine masks and feminine roles.

Figure 60. Detail from a vase probably painted by the ceramist, Achille, c. 400 B.C. In this scene the maid offers a departing warrior the ceremonial cup called patera. She wears a simple, belted tunic which gives the effect of two pieces. The father wears a long, pleated tunic with himation draped over the arm. In the center, every detail of the military costume is evident: the squared cuirass worn over a short chiton, the round shield, crested helmet, and greaves. British Museum, London.

History of Fashions

Figure 61. *Oedipus confronted with the enigma proposed by the Sphinx. This vase painting clearly illustrates the short cloak called the* chlamys. *National Archaeological Museum, Taranto.*

Figure 62. *Detail of frieze in marble from the Parthenon. The men carrying water jars wear a special chiton which did not cover the right shoulder to allow freedom of that arm. It is called* exomide *and was worn generally by the working people. Acropolis Museum, Athens.*

Figure 63. *A statuette from the Hellenistic period of Greek art. This actor wears a long-sleeved tunic with the waistline placed very high in order to make the figure appear taller and more dramatic. The figurine comes from Tanagra, a city of Boeotia, where thousands of small clay figures were discovered in the excavations which began in 1873. Louvre, Paris.*

Figure 64. *Relief of the "Rape of Helen." Judging from the sleeved tunic this work must have been made after Aeschylus (524–456). Museo Profano Lateranense, Rome.*

History of Fashions

Aeschylus proposed the buskins and originated the high waistline for tunics so that actors would appear more important (Figures 63, 64). Then, with Sophocles and Euripides, there appeared on stage a special hairstyle called *onkos,* an archaic style strangely close to the Cretan hairdress (unknown to the Greeks) and which we find again, later, in the Roman theater.

In the Greek comedy, actors wore a *centunculos* (a padded doublet) and comic masks; and they also used grotesque, realistic disguises (Figure 65). On the other hand, actors of the pantomime wore rich costumes and an enigmatic mask, for they were involved only in the movement while other actors did the recitation. From the centuncolos worn by the mimes, with colored patches or spots, the future costume of the clowns would develop.

The Greeks were all conscious of their great civilization and they chose to use dialects of a common language in order to preserve understanding among themselves (Figure 66). Though they had some local difference of cult, they recognized a common pantheon of Olympian deities and, all together, they participated in feasts such as the Olympic games. Despite political separatism, the greater part of Olympic cities united

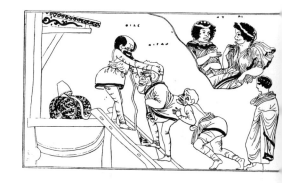

Figure 65. A scene of comedy, from a vase design. The actors are wearing the centunculos *and comic mask.*

Figure 66. Teachers and pupils in a school scene. An unusual vase painting that is important in reporting the life of antiquity. Staatliche Museum, Berlin.

their forces to oppose aggression from other countries. Certainly, the passionate devotion to the *polis* (city-state) was a motive for acts of sacrifice and inspired in the citizen a conscious value of himself, a triumphant art, and a noble generosity. But, in practice, it dissipated the human forces of Greece.

No other style in art has had so great an influence as Greek art. In their love of nature and man, the Greeks idealized the human figure and established laws of beauty which are still generally accepted.

The Greek artists were the first to represent the human figure naturalistically, and they treated even their deities in the same spirit. In the Fifth Century B.C., they created undying canons of beauty. The sculptors and painters were free to abandon conventions established earlier, and they learned to reproduce all that they observed. Moreover, the popularity of gymnastic games created the opportunity to freely observe the nude human figure. This incidental study of nature produced notable results—an idealization and perfection in art. The Greeks, then, created the "classic" style, and the essence of this style is order and form; moderation in design, in expression, and in decoration.

As happens many times in the history of fashions, the perfection and simplicity may become monotonous, or may stir in us a sense of rebellion, a desire to free ourselves from the influence of Greece. Yet, when the liberation is complete, when all fantasies have been explored, we again find new inspiration in that art which in esthetic forms expresses the life of reason.

Greek art is reason revealed. There are no extravagant motifs, no eccentricities of form, no freakish research of novelty; the Hellenes sought only to gather the real essence of things and to represent the ideal possibilities of man.

The Etruscans

About the Twelfth Century B.C., small tribes, whose origin remains one of the fascinating mysteries of history, landed on the virgin coasts of Italy. They settled in a benevolent pine-studded country and called it Etruria. Their center was Tarquinia, but their civilization overflowed the borders of Tuscany. The most brilliant period of development extended from the Eighth to the Sixth Century B.C., when their territory stretched from Capua to the foot of the Alps. The fifth Century saw the beginning of the decline of the Etruscans; and the Third Century marked the end of their independence as they became part of the Roman world, to which they had given the great contribution of their own civilization.

The Etruscans, from contacts with the Greeks of Magna Graecia and vestiges of an Oriental heritage, certainly found a wealth of subjects and themes which they did not fail to exploit, but which they did not always completely understand. Actually, their eclecticism provided them with precious knowledge in the field of pictorial technique and composition; but, happily, it did not overwhelm an originality of tempera-

Figure 67. *Attic kelebe painted c. 470 B.C., from the Tomb of Valle Trebba. The figure in the center is Apollo with his lyre; his splendid costume consists of a long, pleated tunic embroidered at the hem and a rich, triangular cloak. At the right is Mercury with winged buskins wearing a short, light, pleated tunic. Driving the chariot is a goddess in a beautiful tunic. The triangular motif, a special characteristic of the Etruscan dress, is repeated in all of the costumes. National Archaeological Museum, Ferrara.*

ment, which was very different from the Hellenic spirit. In fact, the first settlers of Tuscany drew largely from other cultures, but they did not always find these inspirations congenial to their character.

Notwithstanding the similarities between some Greek and Etruscan productions, we can feel that they are the expression of two different worlds. And thus it is indispensable to make a comparison between Greek and Etruscan art in order to define their relationship. Greek art, in its origins, had drawn from Oriental influences, but very soon it underwent an autonomous evolution, an autonomy that was peculiar to Greek art and followed a progressive development, every phase of which presupposed preexistent traditions. In contrast to this natural and progressive movement, Etruscan art appears very

History of Fashions

Figure 68. *A scene of Europa and the Bull on an Attic vase of the Fifth Century* B.C. *She is wearing a fine, festooned tunic and the typical* eguglion, *a mantle placed obliquely over the tunic; this garment was characteristically worn by Greek priests. The hairdressing is particularly Etruscan in its refinement. Villa Giulia, Rome.*

Figure 69. *This scene of love, framed by a Greek key design, is painted in the bottom of a cup. The young man wears the short chiton with* chlamys *and a straw hat, the* petasos, *hangs on his shoulder. The girl wears a pleated tunic with the* himation *draped over her head. Villa Giulia, Rome.*

independent; its progress always derived from a sort of compromise between inner inspiration and outer influence especially Hellenic, which never ceased to bias it.

Etruscan art continuously recalls the models proposed by the Greek world; but even if Greek influence is always evident, the spirit is definitely Etruscan and Italic (Figures 67, 68). Familiar themes of Greek mythology appear, similar forms and decorative motifs, but all revealing a different spirit. They show an ardor, animation, and a sensual *joie de vivre* that is quite foreign to the moderation of Greek idealism (Figure 69).

Etruscan painting, like Greek painting, was almost exclusively figurative and architectural, but the Etruscans introduced the landscape and other details which appear to be drawn directly from nature.

The Etruscans 71

Figure 70. From Tarquinia, Tomb of the Auguri, this mural presents the interesting costume of the augur priests: earth-colored tunic, black cloak, and dark, felt shoes with pointed toes. Several stylized shrubs of laurel are evident. National Museum, Tarquinia.

Alongside the human figures, one finds schematically and very elegantly designed laurel shrubs (Figure 70). The laurel always had a prominent place in the Etruscan funerary cult and, later, in the Roman rites. It was a custom, in fact, to place bunches of laurel on the tombs, together with olive branches and ivy leaves, in keeping with the popular belief that those evergreens symbolized and assured eternal life.

In contrast to Greek painting, which was exposed to the ravages of time, Etruscan painting has survived for us to see because it was enclosed in tombs. Because their religious belief held the tomb to be the effective house of the spirit, everything for a full and happy life after death was represented on the walls of these vaulted rooms (Figure 71).

Hence we can say not only that the fundamental significance of the paintings is magic-religious, but also that they are an efficacious representation of the Mediterranean environment before the time of Rome.

The Etruscans were expert in ceramic art and their vase paintings show many lively scenes, but we learn of their costume mainly from the unique murals in the tombs of Tarquinia.

The costumes, very similar to the Greek in the general use of the chiton, were different in the choice of colors and in the peculiar disposition of the designs (Figure 72). The designs usually were embroidered because Etruscan women were expert in the art of embroidery as were the Jewish women.

They wore a cloak, called the *tebenna,* which served the same purpose and was quite similar to the himation (Figure 73). For the dance, the tebenna was cut in a special horseshoe shape and worn by women over transparent, embroidered tunics, and by men on the naked body. Dance scenes are widely represented and must have been a favorite form of entertainment.

History of Fashions

Figure 71. *Male dancer wearing the typical, horseshoe-shaped* tebenna. *The cloak seems to be made of pale blue, light-weight linen with the border embroidered in little gold medallions. Tomb of Triclinio, National Museum, Tarquinia.*

Figure 72. *A female dancer wears a tunic of white voile with wine-red designs of dots disposed in groups. She wears an unusual bolero in red felt, or wool, and a necklace. The male dancer wears a turquoise-colored tebenna with a border of dots. On the left we can see a fragment of another feminine figure playing the double flute; over her embroidered voile tunic she wears an atypical overdress of heavy cloth, again in wine red. Tomb of Francesca Justiniani, Necropolis of Tarquinia.*

Figure 73. *Detail of a dance scene showing the dancer wearing a voile tunic embroidered in dark red dots; the typical tebenna is here wrapped in a special, interesting manner. The felt shoes are clearly visible. There are little flowering trees and birds flying in the background; the band of ivy leaves is a typically Estruscan form of ornamentation. Tomb of Triclinio, Tarquinia.*

History of Fashions

Figure 74. *Detail from the archaic Attic Francois Vase. The fishermen wear a singular costume, appearing extraordinarily modern and resembling some beach costumes of today. The lady wears a two-piece dress, composed of the* casula *and the* ependumata, *entirely embroidered in geometrical designs; it is simple and modern in line even though derived from the most archaic form of Greek dress. Archaeological Museum, Florence.*

Figure 75. *An engraved, bronze kysta is representative of Etruscan skill in metal work; the borrowing of a Greek mythology theme is also characteristic. This scene represents the flaying of the silenus Marsyas after challenging Apollo in musical prowess. We see Apollo draped in a rich cloak while his victim is tied naked to a tree. The border of the kysta is decorated with the typical Etruscan motif of stylized leaves and palmettos. Villa Giulia, Rome.*

The Etruscans 75

In musical scenes, Apollo, whom they fêted frequently, is often seen with attractive dancing girls. They are dressed in transparent tunics, exhibiting delightful triangular motifs of draping which characterize the aristocratic Etruscan costume.

Women sometimes are represented in a dress composed of two pieces, perfectly straight and decorated with little dots, geometrically disposed (Figure 74).

For fabrics the Etruscans used wool and linen voile. For some hats and brief corselets and, above all, for shoes (which they wore especially for dancing), they also used felt, as the Cretans and Mycenaeans had done. Indeed, there appears to have been some mysterious liaison in taste with that earlier culture.

Phlyax plays (Farsa Fliacica), a form of burlesque peculiar to Southern Italy, and derived from Greek comedy, prevailed in the Etruscan theater. The farces were made up of parodies and travesties, of which we find many descriptions in vase paintings. The buffoons are always portrayed in their special costume, the centunculos of the Greek pantomime, with designs and applications of grotesque taste in relief.

The Etruscans were a particularly industrious people and lovers of art, but in addition they were able to exploit commercially their particular artistic qualities. Mention should be made here of their remarkable bronze work: sculptures of warriors and animals, bronze *kystae,* and mirrors were produced and richly engraved with delicate skill (Figure 75). The military costume with short skirt, engraved metal cuirass, imposing helmet with a fantastic large crest, and finely finished greaves is particularly well detailed in these sculptures.

The color of their costumes is extraordinarily well preserved in Tarquinia; they used all of the earth colors, from ivory white to wine red, and also some bright yellows and cerulean

Figure 76. *A procession of women carrying water jugs displays the graceful movement and stylized elegance that are typically Etruscan. Black-figure vase. Villa Giulia, Rome.*

Figure 77. *Antefissa from the temple of Apollo at Veii. This was a decoration at the ends of the roof beams. Villa Giulia, Rome.*

blue. The decorative borders on their cloaks were often in contrasting colors, enriched by design motifs derived from the Greeks, but somewhat bolder in taste.

Many paintings and sculptures show Etruscans wearing completely closed, ankle-high shoes; sometimes with pointed toes, and usually in wine-red color. Of course, sandals were worn also.

Etruscans were mainly hunters and fishermen, and it is interesting to see in their paintings the intense polychromy of birds, fish, sea, and rocks, the free and spontaneous forms of all things. Their special character is seen in the expression and movement of their silhouettes which seem to reveal personality: they are anecdotal and graphic, but above all, dynamic (Figure 76). Their personality is expressed, also, in their painstaking search for special colors, a search they never abandoned in their painting, architecture, or costume (Figure 77).

The Etruscans

77

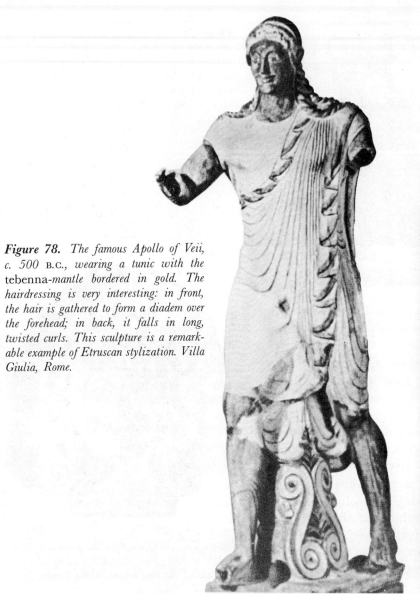

Figure 79. *Head of a goddess in terra-cotta. From the group of Apollo, this head had decorated the Temple of Veii at the end of the Sixth Century* B.C. *Villa Giulia, Rome.*

Figure 78. *The famous Apollo of Veii, c. 500* B.C., *wearing a tunic with the* tebenna-*mantle bordered in gold. The hairdressing is very interesting: in front, the hair is gathered to form a diadem over the forehead; in back, it falls in long, twisted curls. This sculpture is a remarkable example of Etruscan stylization. Villa Giulia, Rome.*

Figure 80. This portrait is surprisingly well preserved both in color and linear detail. The lady, Velia, wears a diadem of golden leaves, held in place by an embroidered band covering the back of the hair. Curls at the sides frame a typically Italian face, recognizable in portraits of following epochs. Tomb of Orcus, Tarquinia.

In the archaic period men wore their hair quite long, as can be seen in the famous Apollo of Veii (Figure 78). Later their hair was arranged in sophisticated curls, some dropping to shoulder length, others appearing "glued" to the forehead in a diadem-like shape. This type of hairdo was common for both women and men, and always left the ears free (Figure 79). Often, aristocratic ladies completed their hairdos with a real diadem in gold (Figure 80).

The Etruscans   79

Figure 81. Necklace of Ruvo. Tiny heads, acorns, lilies, and palmettos cast in gold are interlaced to form this beautiful collar. End of Sixth Century B.C. National Museum, Naples.

Figure 82. Gold bracelets and fibula elaborated with the granulation technique. Archaeological Museum, Florence. Courtesy Vita Italiana magazine.

Figure 83. Bulla; this hollow pin is a splendid example of Etruscan gold work in which tiny spheres are soldered together. *Archaeological Museum, Florence. Courtesy* Vita Italiana *magazine.*

Figure 84. A bulla in laminated gold from Tomb 88A, Valle Pega. Superb example of Etruscan jewelry from the beginning of the Fifth Century B.C. *Archaeological Museum, Ferrara. Courtesy of Professor Nereo Alfieri.*

Extremely clever in goldsmithing, they fashioned singular jewels of stylized elegance (Figures 81, 82, 83). Bracelets, gold pendants, and necklaces in carved amber show an extraordinary level of technical skill and esthetic sensitivity. The gold laminae made into thread or foil were used as the basic element for the creation of jewels; gold foil, embossed, could assume the most varied shapes. But, above all, filigree and granulation techniques enabled the Etruscans, as it had the Greeks, to realize extremely fine ornamental creations. Very fine threads, braided and twisted into chiseled spirals, formed the delicate decoration of jewels. Or, the same gold, fashioned into the tiniest spheres, was laid over the surface to be worked according to the design of the artist (Figure 84).

Etruscan art shows the advent of an aristocratic society with refined but, at the same time, barbaric taste. For its particular view of the world, for the constant tendency to stylize lines and forms, and for the extraordinary sense of movement and color, it developed into a typically Italian art.

Rome

Probably from Alba Longa, in the Eighth Century B.C., a colony of Latins, with a vital need to increase their population, reached the banks of the Tiber and founded the most famous and the most illustrious city in history. To the Latins were joined the Sabines and the Etruscans, who dominated them for a full century before being pushed back, defeated, and absorbed by the Roman world.

From many seeds brought by the winds of changing fortunes, Rome was born. And, while it learned the cult of beauty from the Etruscans and the Greeks, it nevertheless remained fundamentally itself in the essential lines of its life and history.

With the fall of the first monarchy (which constituted a transition), the strong tree of the Roman *res publica,* already having deep roots in the ground, enlarged its shadow along the peninsula: to the North pushing beyond the Alps to take the Gauls, to the South absorbing all of Magna Graecia. It was the Roman Republic and it was called Italy, a name appearing for the first time in history.

Figure 85. *Statue of a Roman woman wearing tunic and* palla. *The* palla *was a cloak worn by women which was very similar to the Greek* himation; *rectangular in shape, it was often draped to cover the head. This woman wears high, open boots and carries two terra-cotta jugs in her hand. National Museum, Naples.*

While the Romans were so occupied with war and politics, Italy was becoming a sort of artistic colony of Greece. The influence of Hellenic culture began early, originally through enslaved artisans and trade exchanges. And the Etruscans, who had enthusiastically adopted so many Greek motifs, spread their popularity among the Romans.

The first Roman code of laws, the so-called Twelve Tables, was engraved in an alphabet made up of Greek and Etruscan elements. And Greek literature was introduced and emphasized by Greek poets, such as Andronicus, living in southern Italy. They translated Greek poetry and drama into Latin, thus opening the dam to the flood of Hellenizing influences: religious, philosophical, political. Romans were not at all averse to accepting the artistic riches of another country; indeed, they were fond of tracing their origins to the legendary arrival in Italy of the Trojan Aeneas and his small band of followers.

With the capture of the Greek city of Syracuse in Sicily, the Romans became aware of the excellence of Greek sculpture and architecture, and they took a liking to the great Greek art. Faithful copies of classic Greek sculptures were made on Roman soil by Greek artisan–slaves.

In spirit, however, the Romans were much closer to the art of the Hellenistic world in which, indeed, they lived. As we have seen, Hellenistic art discarded idealism and the restraint of the classic period and turned, instead, toward naturalism and portraiture.

The history of Roman art had its beginning in the First Century B.C. and was prolonged until the epoch of the Empire. Beautiful are the frescoes at Pompeii, many of which are conserved in the Naples National Museum (Plates 4, 5). Some of them are of bucolic taste; the colors are vivid, with red always dominant; the human silhouettes are gracious in

History of Fashions

Figure 86. A Hellenistic interpretation of a priestess of Isis, recognizable by the sistrum and jug she carries. The draping of her tunic and fringed stole is unusual and graceful. Capitoline Museum, Rome.

themes very often inspired by mythology. The Augustan period marked the golden age in Roman prose and also the highest point in Roman sculpture. At this time architectural relief initiated a new era of spatial conception and anecdotal representation. Roman art became spontaneous and personal during the First Century A.D. When freed from the Greek fascination of beauty in contemplation, it became strong in itself and recognized the individual in his historic reality. In contrast with the simplicity and freedom which appear in Greek art, we see in the Roman a sort of hardness and discipline, strongly self-imposed. The Roman spirit was immersed in reality and in the effort of its representation.

The men and women of Rome wore a tunic very similar to the chiton of the Greek people, differing only in the way it was held on the shoulders. The Greeks used cameos to fasten the material; whereas the Romans preferred some pleats, which created a short sleeve, in place of the clasps. They, too, used girdling to create a bloused effect and to hold in the fullness of the garments; however, the Roman belts were usually visible in women's dresses and were made in embroidered fabric or leather. As with the chiton, the tunic varied in length according to the purpose for which it was used.

The women, in general, wore two tunics and a veil, or cloak, called the *palla* (Figures 85, 86). The Roman brides wore a

Figure 87. Portrait of Giulia di Titus. This is a striking example of an elaborate hairdressing, typical of the Empire period, with curls piled high in front and a chignon of braids in the rear. Capitoline Museum, Rome.

special white tunic with a red cloak, called the *flammeum*, and on the forehead, a little crown of verbena. On their feet, they wore yellow buskins; and that was a sort of homage to the bride for, as we know, the buskins were worn only by very important persons, such as kings, gods, and actors on the stage. A woman who lost a child dressed in blue, and for one year wore no jewels.

Roman women indulged in an elaborate toilette, using cosmetics and perfumes lavishly, and taking a special interest in their hair. They dyed it red with an extract of beets and prunes and sprinkled it with gold powder. In the days of the Republic, the simple, gracious hair styles of the Greeks were in fashion, but during the Empire, coiffures became elaborate with mounds of tight curls and coiled braids (Figure 87). Because they knew the beneficent effect of the sun, they exposed themselves to it; they cared for their bodies as the Egyptian women did, but with a very modern and realistic sense of beauty.

Figure 88. Relief representing a scene of sacrifice. The woman, probably a vestal virgin, is wearing a tunic with high waistline and the palla. The priest, pouring a cup of wine in the fire wears the typical toga and sandal-boots. Vatican Museum, Rome.

History of Fashions

The women of old Rome were not extremely refined, but they were very strong protagonists and examples of dignity, faith, and courage. Unlike their Greek counterparts, they were accorded a position of consequence in the family and in the society.

The typical, beautiful cloak of Roman men was the *toga* (Figures 88, 89). A very large sheet of wool, in its own natural color, was cut into an oval shape. The length, double the height of the person, was folded in two and placed on the shoulders; then each of the two sides was wrapped twice around the body in natural pleats. It gave men a very noble aspect, full of dignity and elegance. All the philosophers, senators, and men of letters wore the toga exclusively and used the deep pleats as pockets.

The simplest and most common toga, in rough wool, was called toga *virilis*. For mourning, a black one was worn, called toga *atra* or *sordida*. Those aspiring to become public officials wore a very white toga, the *candida*, from which the word "candidate" originated. The toga *praetexta* was reserved for governing officials and was used also by actors when they played national tragedies. Young men, when they shaved their first beard, wore the praetexta with solemn ceremony. During the Empire, victorious generals and emperors sometimes wore *coram populo*, the toga *picta* of fine purple cloth, embroidered in gold. The toga *trabea* was reserved for the Augures (priests) who, from the flight of certain birds, divined the outcome of battles; it was a special one, also of purple

Rome

89

Figure 90. A Nineteenth Century interpretation of an ancient Roman shoe shop. The costumes are worn in a manner that looks somewhat Ottocento, but the picture gives us faithful details of a Roman interior and its furnishings. Vocino; Istituto Poligrafico, Rome.

cloth, but long with a train, and fixed on the shoulders. The toga *vitrea,* in transparent voile, was worn only by effeminate men.

For traveling, the Romans wore a very heavy woolen cape, the *paenula,* with a hood (*cucullus*); often, the paenula was made of felt or leather.

Some citizens adopted also, over the tunic, the *lacerna,* the shorter, dark-colored cloak of soldiers. It was fastened with a clasp in front at the base of the neck, and had the same shape as the Greek chlamys.

Sandals and shoes in leather, for men and women alike, were produced in great variety, and their grade of elaborateness often indicated the social status of the wearer (Figure 90).

The basic elements of the Roman costume derived directly from the Greek. The difference was in the detail and refinements (Figure 91).

History of Fashions

The military costume also was modeled on that of the Greeks. The outstanding difference here was in the shape of the shields, which in Greece were round and in Rome quadrangular. The cuirass, much squared in the Greek military costume, partially assumed the form of the chest and body trunk and lengthened in front in an oval shape in the Roman version (Figure 92).

Figure 91. Monochromatic painting on marble from Herculaneum. The women are playing astragali, a Roman game played with the vertebrae of the ram or the small bones of the tarsus. National Museum, Naples.

Figure 92. This fragment of a Roman statue found in the excavations of the Merida Theater, Spain shows details of the Roman military costume of the Empire period. The cuirass is beautifully molded to the natural contours of the torso and decorated with fine bas-relief. Merida Museum.

Figure 93. Fresco representing Iphygenia in Tauride with her handmaidens. First Century A.D. The women wear the tunic with wide clavus down the center and a veil-like palla; they are crowned with laurel. National Museum, Naples.

Breeches and oriental trousers were considered barbarian garb by both the Greeks and Romans; but some Roman troops adopted breeches after fighting in the cold, northern regions.

The cavalry were the elite of the army and they wore belted tunics with two red *clavi* along the hips. The clavi were red stripes decorating the white Roman tunic which, like the toga, was varied, short or long and differently decorated according to the diverse categories of Roman society (Figure 93). Senators, for example, wore a long unbelted tunic with a wide clavus in the center, running from the neck to the hemline. Wide clavi also were worn by other people of high rank of both sexes. Great generals, after a victory, wore a special tunic, called *tunica palmata*, for its decorations of gold-embroidered palm leaves.

In the theatrical costume, also, the Romans imitated the Greeks, the small differences being those of an exaggerated taste (Figures 94, 95). They, too, used the hair style called the onkos, and they wore buskins, but they were higher than those of the Greeks. The national tragedy, the *Praetexta,* was

History of Fashions

Figure 94. Mosaic representing a scene of preparation for comedy. The director wears the toga over his naked body; at his feet, two masks are visible. At the left, two actors present a strange costume of mask and skeepskin skirts. The "actress" playing the flute wears a long tunic with unusual decorations. Another actor puts on a long-sleeved tunic. Agenda Enit 1955.

Figure 95. Hellenistic relief from the First Century B.C. showing the figures of a muse and a comic poet. Lateranense Museum, Rome.

Figure 96. Roman bas-relief in terra-cotta representing Persephone seated with another god. Identified by Romans as Proserpina, she was the wife of Pluto, god of the underworld. They display their personal attributes: the sheaf of grain, the asphodel plant, and the rooster. Persephone wears a tightly pleated tunic covered by the palla, *and on her head a small diadem. Archaeological Museum, Reggio Calabria.*

presented by actors who, as we have mentioned, wore white togas with purple borders. Like the Greeks, they generally used the common Roman dress for the stage. A notable exception was the *bastarda,* an assymetrical tunic created especially for the theater, sleeveless on one side with a long, wide sleeve on the other, which actors liked to use to reinforce their dramatic gestures. In the Roman theater there was not yet a proper costumer, but they did have a person responsible for the care, transportation, and draping of the "costumes."

In the early period, Romans used only white linen or wool dresses, which seems to symbolize the purity of their motives (Figure 96). But, little by little, as their power expanded, that high sense of nobility and austerity, which had characterized the Republican tradition and had determined that special

Figure 97. A Nineteenth Century reproduction of a Roman interior. The lady wears an embroidered tunic in light fabric and high, laced, open boots; her hair is partially enclosed with a golden net. A rich mosaic decorates the floor. Vocino; Istituto Poligrafico, Rome.

Figure 98. *A gold necklace in the form of ivy leaves from Pompeii, First Century* B.C. *National Museum, Naples.*

Figure 99. *Mosaic representing an Auriga, a charioteer, wearing the uniform of the* Fazioni del Circo, *a type of sporting club. From the Imperial villa of Settimio Severo on Via Cassia. National Museum, Rome.*

type of strength with which Rome gained the respect of the world, began to disappear. During the First Century A.D., political corruption invaded Rome; prostitution prospered, and divorce became common. Once reserved Roman women became too free; they used jewels extravagantly and dressed themselves in garments made of transparent fabrics coming from India and China (Figure 97). In that period, the streets of Rome were full of jewelers who made splendid ornaments. Originally, jewels were reserved for the pagan deities, but after a few contacts with the suggestive, fascinating Orient, women learned the excessive pleasure of adorning themselves. And so, earrings, necklaces, bracelets, amulets, precious stones became necessities in their lives (Figure 98).

Though Rome eventually proved unequal to the task of administrating a huge empire, her conquest of the Western world contributed greatly to the advance of civilization. Artistically, Rome's original contributions lie in the fields of architecture and engineering: the creation of the dome and the enclosure of huge spaces; the magnificent bridges, roads, and aqueducts, of which many survive today. But perhaps our greatest debt to Rome is in the realm of law. She established the theory that although the state is supreme, it exercises its power to protect the rights of individuals, groups, and corporations. Even though the powerful privileged class abused the rights of the poor before the law during the Roman Empire, the idea of the Roman *jus* has remained to influence each of our lives.

Christianity offered an international ideology which, in a certain sense, was exacted by the mondial economy of the time. It arrived to express a moral, universal philosophy that was stronger and more influential than stoicism or the Roman law. The new religion gave a significance to the life of the masses who could not be satisfied with the political–social–economic order. Little by little, the people had become convinced of the hopeless nonentity of life on earth, and they eagerly attached themselves to the new spiritual suggestions.

Epicurean Rome had changed every aspect from its once austere beginnings; among majestic palaces, precious possessions, and hundreds of slaves, the sense of *Romanity* was lost (Figure 99).

Although low taste and folly were diffused during that period, the Roman costume did not change in line—only in quality of fabrics and ornamentation. The design of their dress remained the same throughout the centuries, from the first rudimental tunic of the Republic to the refined dress that we admire in the frescoes, all composed in the rhythm and harmony of fine draping. And that purity of line endured until Constantine's epoch when Christianity, officially recognized, made Rome again great and universal.

The Byzantine Period

With affluence in the hands of a few, Roman influence steadily declined until, after 200 A.D., there remained primarily a military state where a once burgeoning civilization had avidly absorbed the Hellenic culture. Diocletian temporarily halted the decay; but he accomplished this only by setting himself up as an absolute monarch, adopting some of the despotic customs of Oriental courts, and making and interpreting the law himself.

The invasions of the Germanic peoples accelerated. To stay their fierce aggression on many fronts, another capital was set up in the East, where Emperor Constantine moved his court in 330 A.D. The site was the ancient Greek city of Byzantium, renamed Constantinople in his honor. Little did he know that he was establishing a seat of government that would outlast Rome by a thousand years! Constantine, however, was to leave an even more permanent mark in history by one of his earlier actions.

Christianity began with a small group of ardent believers after the crucifixion of Jesus in Jerusalem. It was Paul who,

99

with intuitive perception and a genius for organization, transformed a small exclusive sect into a religion that would sweep the world. Christianity had its beginnings in Rome as a little Hebraic sect, where the doctrine of love of Christ and His teachings—which were an example and, at the same time, a promise of resurrection—marked the success of this faith. The religion spread rapidly because it appealed to the downtrodden, the slaves and the laborers, who easily became enamored of those fascinating ideas. Followers were drawn also from the urban middle class which had once been so important economically and politically to Rome, but which was denuded of wealth and influence by the exigencies of the military Empire.

While Christians remained loosely organized in small groups they were tolerated by the Romans, who liberally embraced many foreign religions and pagan cults of mystery. Inevitably, perhaps because of their indomitable belief in the equality of man before God and because they refused to recognize the divinity of the emperor, they incurred his wrath. Beginning with Nero, Christians were often persecuted, as a sort of appeasement to the restless populace. At those periods, they had to gather in secrecy to worship in the catacombs where they buried their dead (Figure 100) but the intensity of their belief made them able to suffer and die for that Christian ideal with an unprecedented strength. When the morally decaying state needed the ideological sustenance of their religion to reinforce its falling power, the Christians were granted some freedom of worship and, in 313, after three hundred years of struggle, Christianity was officially recognized by an edict of the Emperor Constantine. Thereafter, it rapidly expanded throughout the Empire (Figure 101).

Thus, with the new religious ideals which embodied a disdain for wealth and luxury, Roman women again changed their way of life and also their costume. Many decided to strip

Figure 100. Mural painting of a Christian wearing tunic with clavi. *Catacombs of San Callisto, Rome.*

History of Fashions

Figure 101. *Consular diptych of Honorius Flavius (393–424), showing the military costume; on the standard is the sign of Constantine. Cathedral of Aosta.*

off their jewels and give them to the Church. They adopted white, long-sleeved tunics, and sometimes a new type of overdress with sleeves, richly embroidered, and named *Byzantine* for its Oriental flavor. Generally, for mourning, the toga atra was abolished and women who lost their husbands wore tunics in red amaranth.

A new modesty suddenly spread, and Roman men elongated their sleeves and preferred brown or other earth colors for their tunics. In contrast, new importance was given to priests' costumes, which became greatly enriched and extraordinarily pompous.

Many of the early Christians adopted the *dalmatic,* a kind of supertunic, partly open at the sides and usually decorated with ornamental clavi. Later, it was abandoned by the laity and became a regular part of ecclesiastical vestments.

In the catacombs, a simple, rather poor art had developed, built up of many symbols because Christianity was banned. Artists did not care to develop their art as a matter of pride, but rather to express the significance of their faith. In fact, the richness of these paintings derives above all from their inspired expressions. And they are quite remarkable when we consider the dark, secretive conditions under which they were created and the fact that early Christians were generally of the poor, uneducated classes.

Constantine had given to Christianity the impulse and strength of a social revolution. While the old order of imperial power was dissolving, the Church assumed the historical function of creating a new unity. Roman patricians took refuge in the new religion and ideas, and they gave their wealth for the founding of churches and monasteries. The latter became, very soon, the new centers of culture.

In Constantinople, however, the emperors established a court of elaborate elegance and Oriental taste and soon as-

Figure 102. *In this mosaic from San Mauro, Parenzo, the Byzantine ecclesiastical costume is clearly defined. The three figures wear white tunics with vertical red stripes, heritage of the Roman costume. Over his tunic the central figure wears an ample cloak called a casula. Also seen in detail is the interesting Byzantine footgear.*

Figure 103. *This splendid mosaic describing the dance of Salome with the head of St. John shows in detail the sumptuous feminine costume of the Duecento. The close-fitting sleeves of the tunic are embroidered and the ruby-red overdress has skirt and pendant sleeves lined with ermine. Battistero, Venice.*

sumed authority over the Church as well as the state (Figure 102). In the Sixth Century, Justinian established the silk industry and this rare material, richly embroidered, became the foundation of the court costume. Then, for the first time, the design in fabrics was woven on the loom, with splendid backgrounds of red and blue, reinforced by embroideries of gold threads, precious stones, and pearls (Figure 103).

The Byzantine Period

Figure 104. *A detail from the mosaic, "The Tower of Babel." The difference is apparent between the simple, sleeveless tunics of the workers and the sleeved, decorated tunic of the overseer. He also wears leg coverings and the typical Byzantine boots with braided straps; the working men wear simple, laced sandals. St. Mark's, Venice.*

Figure 105. *A mosaic, more informal than the typical Byzantine style, represents the capture of a wild boar. These men wear short tunics with sleeves, decorated by* clavi *like those of the Roman horseman. The shoes, however, are typically Byzantine; very long straps wrap the legs to form a sort of stocking-boot. Piazza Armerina, Sicily.*

Figure 106. *Another mosaic from Piazza Armerina, Sicily, close to Pompeii in spirit. The name "bikini" derives from Bikini Bay in the Pacific which was the theater of early atomic experiments; the women there wore this kind of costume, and the Americans diffused its use in fashion during the first years after World War II. The new word was immediately applied to the girls of Piazza Armerina. This mosaic was actually discovered about 1940.*

The Byzantine costume developed as a strange, rich combination of Roman and Oriental elements: Roman tunics with Oriental designs and embroideries. These tunics were long-sleeved and reached to the floor for women; in general, men of high rank also wore floor-length tunics. The poor men had knee-length tunics and unusual shoes with long straps that wound around the legs to the knee (Figures 104, 105, 106). The tunic was made in many colors, of silk or wool; embroidered borders at the cuff and hemline were common.

The cloak was called the *sagus* and was very similar to the Greek chlamys, which was used also by the Romans. "Sagus" was originally the name of the cloak of the Gauls when they descended into Italy and adopted the Roman costume. The use of it was common to both sexes; longer for the old or notable persons, shorter for the young. It was fixed on the right

The Byzantine Period

shoulder with a fibula or ornamental brooch. A distinguishing feature of the Byzantine sagus was the *tablion,* a rectangular patch in contrasting color placed at the center of the opening, both in front and in back. The tablion fell at the center of the breast because the cloak was worn with the opening at the right side. It was a characteristic of the costume of the royal families and dignitaries, and the tablion of the imperial sagus was elaborated with precious embroidery (Figures 107, 108).

Men wore their hair quite naturally, cut fairly short; and they generally went bareheaded. Women, however, had rigid hairstyles, sometimes resembling a turban with a plump, rolled brim. They were usually constructed with braids interlaced with pearls, ribbons, and precious nets. Over this, the empress placed a rich, gold crown, *kolbak*-shaped and decorated with cascading ropes of pearls, rubies, and emeralds.

With formal dress, men and women wore very long, interesting shoes which appeared in new models and original décolletages covering just the heel and toe. Some of those slippers were embroidered with little flowers in silk. The emperor wore ankle-high silk shoes decorated with pearls; and the empress also had shoes of red or purple embroidered silk (Figure 109).

When Justinian temporarily reunited the East and West Empires, Byzantine splendor flourished in Italy. Early Christian art had seemed to put Rome back again into antiquity with mosaics reviving the ornaments and style of old Pompeii; Byzantine art, however, reflected all the solemnity and etiquette of the court. In San Vitale in Ravenna, the famous mosaics dedicated to Justinian and Theodora are found. Theodora, who earlier had professed a preference for a most debased way of life, became a spiritual leader dominating both the Orient and the Occident as Justinian's empress.

Figure 108. *Mosaic of the Emperor Justinian with his courtiers. Under the imperial* sagus, *we can see the short, elegant tunic of the sovereign; he wears long, red silk hose and fine shoes embroidered in flowers with pearls. The princes at his right wear the sagus with tablion, while the priests are wearing long, white tunics with red clavi. The highest priest wears the green casula and a narrow, white stole with black crosses. All wear similar and typical sandal-shoes. San Vitale, Ravenna, Italy.*

Figure 109. *The Three Magi bearing gifts. The fitted breech-hose are richly embroidered, and the short tunics are draped in an Oriental style. The voluminous cloaks are elaborately decorated, and the singular traveling hats somewhat resemble the Cretan–Mycenaean conical hats while announcing the cowl which follows shortly. Basilica of San Apollinare Nuovo, Ravenna.*

Figure 110. Detail from the Mosaic of Herod. The two kings wear jeweled crowns and narrow, embroidered stoles of the same type as those worn by the priests, indicating a ceremonial dress. Treasury of St. Mark, Venice.

Here she advances from the shining gold background, and she appears to be the purest and saintliest of women in her theatrical, hieratic grandeur (Plate 6). These mosaics describe in detail the costumes of men and women . . . so similar, so rich in ornament, so simple in line.

Every sense of human life is annulled in the Byzantine mosaic and there seems to transpire from the enormous eyes a sense of the Divine, as if human reality is overcome by the supernatural. We cannot see perspective or volume, only a transcendental expression (Figure 110). There is no individuality, only a single model—the Byzantine type—with large, deep eyes to symbolize the soul. These works do not seem to represent men and women, but rather the new spirit of the Christian church.

Ravenna, last capital of the Western Empire, was also the preferred city of the artists in Justinian's time. Hence we find there the richest complex of Byzantine monuments: a profusion of designs and jewels, Oriental in taste, color, and style. All the civil and spiritual world of Constantinople appears in the mosaics of Ravenna. Historical personalities are represented, but their images are neither human nor natural. So closed in sumptuous garments and immobile folds are they that their fixed gaze is hallucinatory, and the Oriental splendor of their hairdos and ornaments renders them similar to idols.

In San Apollinare Nuovo, in Ravenna, a background of radiant gold seems to absorb the procession of virgins carrying crowns; at the same time, it accents the impression of lifelessness and human unreality. The young women wear an overdress, the so-called Byzantine, on the white tunic; and we can observe perfectly the design of the fabric and the embroidered borders, each different from the other (Figure 111).

The most extraordinary embroideries were the Byzantine.

Figure 111. *Famous mosaic of the Procession of Virgins. The young women carry crowns and wear long-sleeved, white tunics, each differently embroidered with a broad stripe in the center which conserves the line of the Roman clavus. The overdress, the so-called* Byzantine, *is presented with diverse designs and decorations. Basilica of San Apollinare Nuovo, Ravenna.*

Figure 112. *This precious fabric, sent as a gift to Charlemagne by Pope Adriano, was created c. 700 A.D. Typically Byzantine is the brocade as well as the geometrical designs grouped to form borders. The perfection of Byzantine weaving produced clearly defined shapes on backgrounds which were almost exclusively red. Victoria and Albert Museum, London.*

Figure 113. *Famous cross of Agilulfo, who reigned from 591 to 616 after Theodolinda. It is representative of the best of Byzantine jewels. Treasury of San Giovanni di Monza.*

Figure 114a. *Mosaic representing Noah's Ark. Noah, after arranging the last birds, assists his three sons and their wives. St. Mark's, Venice.*
Figure 114b. *Detail of the same mosaic. Byzantine mastery of mosaic technique is evident in the grace of the birds, shaded in delicate tones of pink, lilac, blue, gray, and black.*

a

b

Many artisans occupied a lifetime in the creation of a splendid technique that lasted for centuries. Most of these monuments of embroideries were dedicated to kings and queens, or made for the costumes of the high clergy. A famous example, in Reims, was a room prepared for Queen Jeanne of Bourgogne, decorated with thirteen hundred parakeets embroidered in gold and five hundred sixty-one butterflies with wings embroidered in gold, a perfect reproduction of the Queen's coat of arms. Countless other examples give testimony to the prodigious Byzantine textile art (Figure 112).

In all the cities, as well as its capital, the Byzantine Empire left excellent works in ivory, ceramic, wood, gold, and stones (Figure 113). Artisans produced thousands of precious objects such as jewels, pendants, and golden cups; blue cups in glass were decorated with flowers, birds, and arabesques. They were especially gifted in miniatures and mosaics. In the palaces and villas of Constantinople, in the temples along the coast— everywhere—art and religion were united in the common aspiration of grandiosity. Never was art so closely tied to a tradition and culture (Figures 114, 114a). The state lasted eleven centuries, but the art still lives today; original art—rigid, aristocratic, and cold—a style interrupted by Giotto who dedicated himself to the study of man in his natural expressions.

Besides a unique style, the Byzantine civilization preserved and transmitted the Roman jus and the classic texts of literature, science, and philosophy, which might have been lost forever during the "Dark Ages" that had descended upon the West.

The Middle Ages

The barbaric darkness descended chiefly over the Gauls of Caesar and over Spain and Italy. Gaul was divided among the Frankish tribes, occupying the Rhine country, and the Visigoths and Burgundians of the South, who considered themselves independent after the fall of Rome. The north-western part, still nominally under Roman domination, was first invaded by the Merovingians.

Merovingian means "sons of the sea;" and, indeed, they were not only barbarians but also pirates. They occupied the country around Soissons, then all of Brittany, and established one of the less noble dynasties of history, which lasted for two centuries. At the beginning of the Fifth Century, Gaul was partitioned into a multitude of small, quarreling kingdoms ruled by a vast clique of piratical successors. One of them, Chilperic, became notorious for his cruelty, his robberies, and his crimes to the point of being called the Nero and Herod of his time.

Those kings, later identified as *rois fainéants,* respected the clergy for its wealth and learning and hastened to recog-

113

nize Christianity. Perhaps for this reason, the unworthy Chilperic was honored at his death and was covered with a sumptuous mortuary pall made in a monastery of Soissons. It was embroidered with three hundred golden bees and a gold cross fashioned with precious stones.

In the Eighth Century, however, a new blood line rose to power. Pope Stephen II, coming from Rome to Gaul in 753, crowned Pepin "The Short" as king of the Franks and thereby established the great dynasty of the Carolingians. In 768 Pepin died and was succeeded by his son Charlemagne, the greatest and wisest monarch of the Middle Ages; he was not only a warrior, but also a staunch and sincere propagator of Christianity.

The resulting close cooperation between the State and the Church was, indeed, one of the more brilliant ideas of political history and was climaxed by the transformation of Charlemagne's kingdom into the Holy Roman Empire, which was to have the prestige and the power of Imperial and Papal Rome.

This significant event represented a brilliant interlude in medieval darkness. It could have put an end to illiteracy three centuries before Abelard of France and Dante of Italy, if the succeeding kings had continued the great work initiated by Charlemagne. The Holy Roman Empire was a noble conception of order in a world injured by barbarity and violence.

When the invasions began, the clothing of barbaric peoples was not very interesting; they simply protected themselves from the cold with skins of animals and rudimentary breeches. Because they were so menacing, their helmets seemed to be aggressive weapons rather than protective armor. Fascinated by the Roman tunic and toga, the invaders adopted them immediately; and very soon they assimilated that sense of elegance which made them able to participate in the general evolution that would create the beautiful European costume.

Figure 115. Detail from the mosaic, "The Beheading of St. John the Baptist": Salome presenting the head to King Herod. Although the story took place in Christ's time, it was illustrated here by an artist of the first half of the Fourteenth Century who portrayed the protagonists wearing costumes of the Thirteenth Century. Salome wears a long tunic with fitted sleeves and an overdress with wide sleeves bordered in ermine. The dalmatic of Herod is splendid, embroidered with precious stones. The dress of Herodias, mother of Salome and second wife of Herod, is finely embroidered and typically Thirteenth Century. St. Mark's, Venice.

For many centuries more the Byzantine style would influence Christian art throughout the world (Figure 115). But Charlemagne was crowned in Rome, and in the art and costume of Western Europe an attempt was made to return to and renew the old Latin forms. This revival was to remain as the basis of the Romanesque style of the future.

The Middle Ages 115

Figure 116. Miniature painted on an already used parchment showing a regal personage—possibly King Arthur. Manuscript of Walther von der Vogelweide. Württemberg Library, Stuttgart.

History of Fashions

Latin had become the chief literary language of Europe because it was the speech of the Roman conquerors and the official language of government. Then, in the Third Century, it became the official language of the Church, which accounts for its survival during the Dark Ages. The early monastic scholars, many of them of the Benedictine Order, copied pagan Roman literature and preserved it in the monastery libraries. Monks were the only learned men—even the aristocracy generally had become illiterate—and education was attendant upon spiritual enlightenment. Charlemagne recognized the desperate need for schools and made an effort to establish them at monasteries throughout the empire; at his famous Palace School he gathered the finest scholars from England and the continent. The miniatures and illuminated manuscripts produced by the monks of Ireland played a great role in the "Carolingian Renaissance" and they remain a unique artistic heritage from that period (Figure 116).

At the time of Charlemagne, silk weaving, embroidery, and appliqué work were practiced throughout Europe. Later, when this artistry became highly developed, it was customary to embroider dresses with writing, recounting holy or profane stories, and even illustrating songs. They would complete the words of a song with a design of musical notes (which had a square form at that time), embroidered in gold and filled with four pearls.

From Einhard, Charlemagne's biographer, we learn that the Emperor generally wore the Frankish costume consisting of linen shirt and breeches, silk tunic, and a blue cloak. He wore hose fastened by bands wrapped around his legs, and shoes, which on feast days were adorned with precious stones. In the cold of winter he wore a close-fitting fur coat under his cloak. Long, red linen hose, bound with thongs, were worn by most of the men of the royal court, and sword belts girdled their tunics or shorter linen shirts.

Feudalism established definite class differences and, naturally, these appeared in the costume. Men of the lower classes wore simple tunics and breeches, while the noblemen dressed in very rich garments with long, embroidered sleeves. They wore large, elegant cloaks, many jewels, and fine shoes that unfolded around the ankle like the petals of a flower (Figure 117).

Wealthy ladies had embroidered dresses with jeweled cuffs at the wrists and precious belts on the hips. The length and richness of the dress varied according to the social status. The same simple line, semifitted in the bodice and flaring at the hem, was common to the women of all classes, but the simple people used cruder fabrics in wool or cotton with primitive, ingenuous motifs of decoration; modesty appeared also in the drab colors they used.

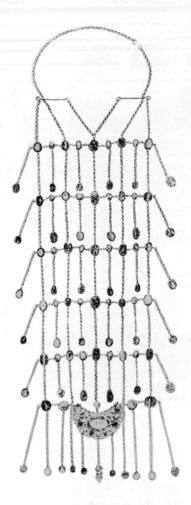

Figure 118. Splendid necklace covering the breast which belonged to the Empress Giselle, c. 1000. It is a beautifully crafted work made of little, golden chains and precious pendants in diamonds, emeralds, and sapphires. Staatliche Museum, Berlin.

Costume in the Middle Ages in France, Spain, Italy, and Middle Europe was considered the symbol of economic and official status. The kings, in fact, distinguished themselves with ever new refinements; and there are preserved in many museums numerous precious cloaks that belonged to famous sovereigns. At feudal courts, noblemen and ladies reached such high levels of refinement that there developed a veritable "game" of elegance. Ladies wore finely decorated dresses with jeweled belts and long, wide sleeves. Their long hair was often braided with ribbons or enclosed in long tubes of silk or leather. And they adorned themselves with splendid necklaces (Figures 118, 119). Men, too, wore sumptuous jewels: earrings, necklaces, bracelets, and rings.

Dresses were made of wool, linen, sometimes leather, and completed with fine elements of decoration: embroidery, precious jewels, and fur. Ermine was the most fashionable fur, but sable and otter were popular too, and cloaks were sometimes designed with cowls and short *pèlerines*.

The medieval people always presented an astonishing variety and originality in physical type, as well as in the color

Figure 119. *This necklace is part of the Visigothic treasure. It is of enameled gold with embedded precious stones. Bucharest Museum. (Left.)*

and taste of their costumes. Men surpassed women for the magnificence and vivacity of colors and styles. Usually, the dresses were woven, cut, and sewn at home. Only affluent people had professional tailors, who in England were called "scissors." The décolletages and the hems were almost always ornate with fur.

The "mortar," flat and square, was the hat used by scholars at the end of the Middle Ages, and its form still persists in the ceremonial costume of most American universities.

The culture of the Scandinavian peoples also reached a high level of artisanry in the centuries between 700 and 1000. Beautiful jewels from that mysterious epoch were recovered from Viking ships during the excavations of the last century and the beginning of this century (Figure 120). Those ships functioned as large sepulchral monuments, in which kings were buried with all their riches, arms, and jewels. Other excavations brought to light typically feminine jewelry: necklaces, pendants, and charms in gold, silver, and precious

Figure 120. Necklace made of thirty-four pendants of bronze with silver plaques, c. 900. State Historical Museum, Stockholm. (Above.)

The Middle Ages

121

Figure 121. *Stained glass windows from the Church of St. Ouen at Rouen. The woman's head is modestly coiffed in linen while the man's hat is apparently a soft beret. Both wear draped cloaks with decorative borders over their tunics.*

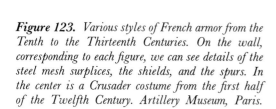

Figure 122. Miniature from the Codice Chigiano representing a battle toward the end of the Middle Ages. Here are typical military costumes and shields decorated with different coats of arms. Vatican Library, Rome.

Figure 123. Various styles of French armor from the Tenth to the Thirteenth Centuries. On the wall, corresponding to each figure, we can see details of the steel mesh surplices, the shields, and the spurs. In the center is a Crusader costume from the first half of the Twelfth Century. Artillery Museum, Paris.

stones. Glass chessmen reveal the popularity of a game obviously learned from their expeditions to the Orient.

The fusion of glass with color, known as stained glass, is an art that was born in France about the Seventh Century. Although the art of painting glass was known, as we have seen, in antiquity, it was used primarily in the form of crushed glass for decorative effects. But glass really was not used as a representative art until 980, when the Archbishop Adelbert of Reims adorned his cathedral with windows. In 1190 the monk Theophile, an expert in that art, described extensively its technique: the panes were designed and painted, baked in an oven to fix the color, and then put together by grooved strips of lead. In Byzantine art, painters and artisans sought to reproduce polychromatic effects in mosaics. Therefore, from already existent techniques, a new form of expression was initiated in stained glass, which later would be widely adapted—especially in the Thirteenth Century. The ultimate aim was to color the interior of the churches with mystic light and a convincing intensification of the Christian spirit (Figure 121).

With the descent of the barbarians into Italy, there came also the shades of legends, myths, and fears, creating a general confusion between culture and belief, North and South, Orient and Occident. It culminated in the terror of the Apocalypse, supposedly forecast for the year 1000, that seemed to stop all evolution and petrify the world. Even Christian moral strength vacillated, and all prayed for Divine protection in dread of the end of humanity. Now, once again, jewels and elegance were easily renounced (Figures 122, 123).

Just after the year 1000, and perhaps because of the recent sad experiences, difficulties, and contrasts, all the people rediscovered old heritages of liberty and faith with which they built the foundations of a new European evolution.

The Age of Romanesque Art

The barbarians had passed without leaving new elements of grace but finally there were better days after the long, dark night that preceded the arrival of the year 1000. The Romanesque arts spread throughout the lands where, in antiquity, the Eagle of the Roman legions had ruled. The world seemed to find itself, and the whole of civilization revived. Life began again with renewed pleasure, and new horizons opened for art, government, and costume. In this reawakening, it seems that a sort of miraculous leaven of memories moved the ground and, from all the old Roman trunks, new sprouts germinated everywhere.

Although in painting there remained some influences of Greek–Oriental art—human forms without elegance, floral and geometric decorations—in architecture a new style was born, called "Romanesque" for its close ties with old Roman forms. From the end of the Roman Empire to the beginning of the Eleventh Century there had been no new architectural developments; churches and all art forms remained strongly influenced by the Byzantine style. In the Eleventh Century,

Figure 124. *The figure on the left is a sculpture of the Queen of Sheba from Notre Dame de Corbeil. She shows the new line of costumes begun in the Twelfth Century and continued into the Thirteenth. Her characteristic long braids are wrapped in ribbons; often, at this time, braids were enclosed in embroidered silk tubes. The dress has a simple, fitted bodice with a soft, full skirt falling in natural folds; the double sleeves are very wide and are finished at the edge with* merlons. *Louvre, Paris.*

Figure 125. A stucco decoration in the chapel of Santa Maria in Valle shows the character of the female costume in Romanesque times. The Byzantine tradition is continued in the heavily embroidered overdresses of the two figures on the left, while the wide sleeves are typically medieval. The crown worn on smooth, center-parted hair is a customary addition to the costume. The third figure wears a simpler, pleated dress and is wrapped in a hooded cloak. Cividale, Friuli.

European architecture became the tangible expression of a monastic culture. It began to liberate itself from the oppressing materials and ostentatious colors of the East, finding a powerful spiritual dignity in the simple and pure arcades of the Romanesque cathedrals.

Characteristic of Romanesque art was a certain popular spirit. Nature and man returned to life, and the new style corresponded to a general renewal of figurative vision. A fresh vigor was apparent as the paintings and sculptures portrayed the works and the days of men; many allegoric figures in soft costumes looked out from the naves, calling the attention of the world to human expression (Figures 124, 125).

The Age of Romanesque Art   127

Figure 126. *Frederick II of Swabia, Emperor of the Holy Roman Empire from 1215 to 1250, wears a soft, silk tunic with velvet cloak; falling in front, like a Roman clavus, is a preciously embroidered stole. Biblioteca Ambrosiana, Milan.*

The first two hundred years after 1100 were the golden centuries of the Middle Ages which prepared the world for a new epoch of civilization (Figure 126). To understand the importance of this period we must look for a moment at history, because any study of clothing without that of the ethics and history that distinguish it in time is tantamount to speaking of men as dolls.

From the ruins of feudalism sprouted the most original flower in Italian life: the free commune. Grafted on hidden Roman roots, it fought for existence and won its freedom from feudal lords, becoming a notable part of the history of Italy. Indeed, one of the most significant developments of the Middle Ages was the rise of towns all over Europe, involving a social revolution and creating a new class of people: the bourgeoisie. The town was founded on commerce and trade, but it became the center of medieval culture and with it the evolution of Western civilization took a giant stride forward.

Against the cupidity of nobles, dominating local territories from their castles, the working people in the Latin cities defended the ideal of a proper justice. So the towns were granted charters that guaranteed them the right of self-government. The Roman jus was resurrected and Christianized in canonic laws and communal statutes.

Together with the ideals of liberty, there was an eagerness for the diffusion of knowledge, regarded as a necessity of life and progress. Therefore new universities were created in the cities and they became the centers of the new culture. The first was the University of Bologna, then came that of Paris, where Abelard established the logical method of Aristotle as the indispensable tool of learning.

Religion in the Middle Ages was the omnipresent subject in every manifestation of life: in politics and war, in art and culture, and in the theater and costume.

History of Fashions

The "Holy Wars," the Crusades, were begun in 1095 at the urging of Pope Urban II. They lasted for two hundred years and had a tremendous influence on the emergent taste of the medieval populace. Exotic foods, fabrics, and items of luxury were brought back by the warriors, stimulating trade and new methods of finance.

The costume of the crusader consisted of a suit of chain mail, a large helmet that reached to the shoulders with slits for the eyes, and a tall, heart-shaped shield. Shoes were of steel with mobile metameres; and over the armor was placed a tunic called the *cotta,* often sleeveless and open at the sides, or slit down the front and back of the skirt for ease of riding. Apparently, it was used as a protection from the sun's glare on the polished armor, but it served also as identification, for the knight's military order was emblazoned on the front and back. This was the beginning of the widespread use of heraldry in the Middle Ages (see Figure 123). The crusaders also carried the *aumônière,* a little pouch for alms hanging from their belts, and created a fashion the ladies were to adopt (Figure 127).

Figure 127. *A miniature of the Thirteenth Century from the poem "Eneite" of Heinrich von Veldeke. We see that it is a bloodless tournament because the protagonists wear ordinary tunics instead of cuirasses and their lances are blunted with leather balls. From "L'Epoca della Fede," Staatsbibliothek, Berlin.*

The theater was essentially religious and was absorbed by the Church for its edifying value. The theatrical costume was the ecclesiastical dress of the epoch: actors donned episcopal dress when playing the prophets and papal robes when acting God. For representations of the Holy Family, they resorted to the Hebraic costume and added wings to the flowing tunics for the angels. Symbolic colors were used also to designate characters and scenes. The liturgical drama, which found its highest expression in the lauds and laments of Jacopone da Todi, ended with the medieval world; and from the holy drama, the theater passed to the Renaissance feasts.

From the monasteries came general progress in the arts, great and small. At times it was amazing—as, for example, the embroidery executed by inspired and humble nuns with prodigious patience and taste. Ceremonial cloaks were of purple silk, embroidered with gold thread and precious stones.

In clothing, the Byzantine influence was overcome in the attempt to rediscover the human figure and to restore natural movement and grace. All seemed in harmony with this renewal of the costume, but each people put its own stamp and personal accent on the forms. In France, for example, ladies wore multicolored dresses and trained their hair with colored ribbons. English women preferred delicately embroidered floral decorations as a border. The Spanish, on the contrary, used great contrast of color and combined Latin simplicity with Arabic preciosity. In Germany, where earlier a very simple and primitive costume had prevailed, the Twelfth Century marked the beginning of real elegance; women wore gold circles around the forehead, and hair fell on the breast where the dress showed a comely décolletage and a fine fastening. The Russians, still feeling the Byzantine influence, wore the typical kolbaks (the tall fur hats), dresses in brocade, and shoes in fur.

Figure 128. *A miniature from the* Manessischen Liederhandschrift *shows German costumes of the Fourteenth Century with the typical sleeveless overdress. Heidelberg University Library.*

For all Europe, the feminine costume became lighter, more fitted, and a little more graceful. Especially interesting were the *coiffes,* or headgear, which adorned the face as well as the head, almost always draping the neck and often the chin too (Figure 128). The term "coiffe" from the Middle Ages, indicates generally all the kinds of feminine hats which were

The Age of Romanesque Art 131

Figure 129. *A statue of St. Cecile shows the customary hairstyle for women: very long hair braided with ribbons or encased in embroidered silk tubes. Castelvecchio Museum, Verona.*

made in linen; they were worn over a little cap, white or black, fitted to the head. The origin of the coiffe was a sort of bonnet adorned with various bands or ruffles, and it changed its name according to its particular shapes. In fact, the coiffe was called *cornette, guimpe,* or *barbette* according to whether it had "horns," pleated wings, or light voiles that passed under the chin, draped in front, and often reached to the breast. This barbette originated the headdresses of many religious costumes and, later, the various forms of the *touret.*

Noble girls often wore their hair falling on the shoulders or put up in very long braids. Sometimes the braids were enclosed in long tubes of embroidered silk; at other times the hair was gathered in gold nets, known as the *crespine.* Finally, stylized diadems or circlets of gold frequently completed the hairdos (Figure 129).

Usually the dress was accented by a belt, often girdling just the hips, below which the soft skirt flowed to the floor (Figure 130). Sometimes the belt was decorated and held in the center by a precious buckle from which it continued down the skirt. The first kind of purse for ladies then appeared; the so-called *scarsella* was adopted from the crusaders' *aumônière* and hung from the belt in a similar fashion. The sleeves were extremely wide and sometimes had ornamental borders; usually they exposed the fitted sleeves of a white shirt always worn under the dress.

Shoes were pointed and flat, in silk-satin or felt. Men generally wore light boots made out of felt with leather soles. Sometimes the leather soles were placed on the bottom of the stockings, which were actually a combination of breeches and hose, and for which red was the preferred color.

On that base, which would be common and widely adapted for centuries, men wore a long tunic, called the *zimarra.* For the horsemen, the zimarra was open in front; this ensemble

Figure 130. *Miniature from the so-called* Codice di Adone *indicates that the feminine dress was sometimes worn belted and had a train. Sleeves, very wide at the wrist, were either heavily embroidered or lined with* vair. *Long hair falls over the shoulders, and pointed shoes complete the costume. Cremona Cathedral.*

Figure 131. This angel is attributed to the Maestro della Maddalena, c. 1280. Hair interbraided with colorful ribbons and surrounding the head turbanlike creates a harmonious contour for the feminine face. Church of San Michele, Rovezzano, Florence.

History of Fashions

was used frequently by medieval nobles for hunting. A leather belt with metal boss held the zimarra at the waistline, and bracelets with similar motifs often decorated the wrists and upper arms.

It was fashionable to wear gloves, and the falconer wore one glove longer than the other on the bird-carrying hand. Horsemanship was also considered an elegant accomplishment for the aristocratic ladies and they liked to accompany the gentlemen in the hunt.

Men also wore short pèlerines with cowls, which were completely embroidered and were called the *chaperon*. Cowls and pèlerines that were not embroidered were worn by magistrates, as well as by men of letters, over a special long tunic called the *guarnacca*.

The *scapular* was a special garment derived from the Hebraic ephod which knights sometimes wore; it was open at the hips, closed at the neck by a collar strip, the *pistagna*, and on the breast were embroidered the insignias of the orders to which they belonged. The first garb of monks consisted of a long, unbelted tunic and a kind of short scapular, which often ended with a cowl.

In the Italian republics, life was intense in the corporations of trade guilds, in costume, in the arts and handicrafts. Venice was the port through which many of the luxuries of the East flowed and great numbers of artisans were employed in producing all the fineries of costume: gloves, shoes, ribbons, buckles, furs, and jewels. But Florence was becoming the real center of the new movement and civilization that was laying the foundations for the great Italian Renaissance (Figure 131). Its artistic primacy derived from enterprise in commerce and banking and a dedicated specialization in the trades. In Florence, in fact, every stonecutter became an architect, every jeweler became a sculptor, and the most unpretentious player of the guitar became a composer. Minstrels appear frequently in Florentine scenes dressed in bizarre costumes decorated with stripes, merlons, and little bells.

At the end of the *Duecento* and the beginning of the *Trecento,* Florence was a furnace of ardent political struggles, but at the same time it had conceived the beginning of a very fine society. And while the lower classes were diverted by grotesque representations of the "Eternal Life," the nobles preferred to prepare feasts of high taste.

Work and combat, poetry and love, mingled in that untiring city, divided and torn by interior struggles but united in its ideal of beauty, which imprinted on it forever the seal of aristocracy.

The Fourteenth Century

While Romanesque art preferred to represent even Christ as a crowned king, wearing precious embroidered cloaks that hid all human form, Gothic art tended to draw away from the hieratic absence of movement and the cold immobility of the body. Gothic art discovered again both individual expression and softness of gesture.

Cimabue's madonnas were still Byzantine, but his rebellious feelings toward a stifling tradition probably helped to mold the genius of Giotto. Angelotto di Bondone, known as Giotto, was able to throw off the pervasive Byzantine influence and personalize the new art. He created a new kind of picture space with his majestically simple yet realistic figures, permanently altering the artistic vision of the western world (Figures 132, 133).

From Giotto and Dante was born the impulse to give the human spirit a free and swift rhythm in every field of art and knowledge. In their unique, personal expressions these men offered the world a new, fundamental, and universal concept of humanity. This century seemed to be imbued with a new spirit and hope.

Figure 132. *Detail from "San Gioacchino fra i Pastori," a painting by Giotto (1266–1336). The precise line of the belted tunic and the simple cloak worn by the shepherds are shown here in delicate, pastel colors. Cappella degli Scrovegni, Padua.*

Figure 133. *A detail from Giotto's "Resurrection of Lazarus." This tunic is particularly interesting for the special cut of the sleeves and the unusual fastening. Cappella degli Scrovegni, Padua.*

Figure 134. *Miniature showing Henry of Luxembourg receiving the keys of a city, which may be Asti. The soldiers wear interesting military costumes, and all of the horsemen wear cloaks that allow free movement of the arms. Various heraldic banners are displayed. Behind the king, we see a crowned woman—probably the queen. From Codex Balduini, Staatsarchiv Koblenz.*

Figure 135. *Detail of a fresco by Giovanni da Milano revealing some fine fashions of the Fourteenth Century. The figure on the left wears a dress made of velvet and the famous* panno d'oro *(golden cloth) fabricated in Italy. The other lady displays an interesting and elegant costume made of two different tunics; the overdress is light and transparent. Church of Santa Croce, Florence.*

As Gothic architecture was the expression of lofty aspirations, so the costume found elevating lines full of grace. Art, leaving behind the static forms, strove for movement and harmony (Figure 134), and the costume, too, seemed to be vivified, becoming delicately enriched in line, with changing details, colors, and fabrics. Following the motif of the Gothic arch, the human image seemed to be designed as a taller, more slender figure (Figure 135).

The rise of the Seignories encouraged the development of games of elegance, refinement, and a studied cultivation of the arts. *Mecenatism* (a culture of patronage) made possible, and easier, the exploitation of personalities and gave vigor to all the creative strength of man.

One may ask why Italy first felt this reawakening. It was because the old Roman world never was completely destroyed, and because classic art survived in Rome, Verona, Mantua, Padua, and Florence. The Latin language still lived in the new Italian tongue, which seemed to be only a musical variant. Furthermore, there were more cities and industries in Italy than in the other countries of Europe; Italy was never really subjected to the extremes of feudalism, and its nobility came to depend on the cities and the merchants (Figure 136). The enterprises of merchants were varied, and their shops for import and export of the most diverse hand-manufactured articles always were picturesque and active centers of city life.

In addition to their commercial activities, the great merchant families of the Fourteenth Century engaged in the art of weaving which was held in high regard. Artist-artisans, extremely knowledgeable in technique and possessing great imaginative taste, created new kinds of fabrics and designs of Oriental character. They were probably introduced to Sicily by Arabs; and from Sicily, they were further elaborated and refined by the Italian manufacturers who flourished every-

Figure 136. *A French bourgeoise of the Fourteenth Century. Her dress with fitted bodice is belted at the waist with a ribbon from which a rosary dangles. The wide, turned-back sleeves of the overdress reveal the typical* manchettes *of the shirt. Her coiffe is of a type that will remain in style for about three hundred years. Gaignières Collection, Bibliothèque Nationale, Paris.*

Figure 137. *From the Nativity of the Virgin Mary, a Thirteenth Century mural in the Pinacoteca of Siena, we have two attendant ladies dressed in red and blue showing an elegant, slim, and simple line.*

Figure 138. A bourgeois from Châlons-sur-Marne. He wears a tunic with fitted, buttoned sleeves and an overdress with a cowl. Dorelots, little curls, escape from his linen coiffe. *This was a popular French fashion for men in the Thirteenth and Fourteenth Centuries. Gaignières Collection, Bibliothèque du Roi, Paris.*

where, especially in Tuscany and Venice. Velvet, very fashionable in this century, was produced primarily in Genoa where it became famous (Figure 137).

The varied style of clothing, particularly that of men, gave added importance to the profession of tailoring, since it called for particular skill. The breech hose were no longer worn under the men's tunics. Stockings were fitted and elegant, and tied to the breeches with tapes. Soled stockings, with sharp points, echoed the architectural style of "flamboyant" Gothic, with its lancets and spires. The outlined hems of sleeves also were characteristic of the architectural taste of this century as they repeated the motif of *tour merlons* (tower battlements). The points of the shoes and of the soled stockings were stuffed with horsehair.

The eccentricity in male clothing of this period was exemplified particularly in the headgear, which was quite varied and fanciful. Sometimes it was composed of two pieces so that it was possible to wear rich and tall hats on top of the coiffe or cowl. Men did, in fact, wear linen coiffes with which they sometimes created unusual styles; as, for example, the *dorelots*—a French hairdo consisting of little curls coming out from linen caps (Figure 138).

The Fourteenth Century   143

Figure 139. Pierre de Carville, Lord-Mayor of Rouen, wearing two tunics. The skirt of the under tunic is lined with vair, as are the sleeves of the overdress. Gaignières Collection, Bibliothèque Nationale, Paris.

In France both men and women lined their coats with white and gray *vair* (the fur of a kind of squirrel), in a floral design depicting lilies (Figures 139, 140). The French feminine costume introduced deeper décolletages and the ladies liked to wear trains and have men carry them. They inaugurated, too, a sort of two-piece dress: long skirts in color and a jacket down to the hips.

English ladies favored a complex garment: a jacket of special cut, often inlaid with heraldic designs, was fitted in front but fell capelike from the shoulders in back; the collar and cuffs were trimmed in ermine and other furs. The English men, instead, wore tight-fitting waistcoats, simply and elegantly cut, sometimes closed with buttons, and always with embossed silver belts (Figure 141).

In Italy, men used many large, precious buttons, and little purses, like the feminine scarsella, hung from the belt; both articles were very refined in styling and gave importance and dignity to the costume. Some purses were in velvet with pearl buttons, and even decorated with heraldic motifs embroidered in gold, or wrought in gold and enamel and appliquéd.

Figure 140. *Detail from the* Crocifisso Bardi *showing a group of ladies dressed in the fashionable style of the Thirteenth Century. Cloaks and dresses were often lined with fur, but vair was a particular favorite because contrasting effects of black and white could be obtained with inlaid work; usually the pattern imitated the shape of a lily. That fashion became the symbol of affluence and aroused the strong censure of the Church; sumptuary laws limited the use of vair to knights and their ladies. Church of Santa Croce, Florence.*

Figure 141. *An old print illustrating English masculine costumes of differing social classes under the reign of Edward III, c. 1350.*

Figure 142. Portrait of Francesco Petrarca by Andrea del Castagno, great Florentine painter (1390–1457). The poet wears the typical guarnacca which, beginning with the Thirteenth Century, was the preferred costume of men of learning. Cenacolo of Sant'Apollonia (from the Villa Pandolfini of Legnaia), Florence.

Venice was the most celebrated center for the manufacture of eyeglasses, which at that time consisted of two big round lenses placed astride the nose in a leather frame—not too unlike the style many young people affect today.

The *pellanda* was an ample tunic; worn with a cowl or headgear, it was used especially in town and was not removed even when greeting someone. The learned and the old were usually faithful to traditional styles and preferred to wear large, majestic cloaks, often fur lined.

The guarnacca, in general reserved for the intellectuals, was also used by the high society, including magistrates and physicians, and, in Florence, even the merchants (Figure 142). The guarnacca was worn over the short tunic, which, in the Italian republics, was called *gonella*. At the university, students were wont to wear a black guarnacca, and the "magnificent" Rector wore a crimson cloak bordered in ermine.

The Doge of Venice had a unique costume in yellow brocade, a short pèlerine in ermine, and the famous rigid, dogal bonnet, pointed on the forehead.

Gloves still conserved a symbolic value, and they were used by chiefs of state as insignia of authority. It was proper to offer a pair of gloves in return for a favor done. In the middle of the century, it was customary to present a chamois glove to the bridegroom leading his bride to the altar on a horse, for chamois gloves were the most expensive. Others were made of wool, and still others of cotton for summer use. Italian gloves were the most appreciated, but in Spain and in France, too, many glove industries flourished.

The pointed beards that adorned men's chins seemed in harmony with their pointed shoes, sleeves, cowls, and the Gothic arches. Really, men's care for their beards and hair was, at that time, a sort of mania engrossing the young and not-so-young. It all seems to confirm how the people of that

History of Fashions

century were exceedingly sensitive to the search for elegance and the need to feel and follow their time.

Fashion introduced applications on the dress of geometric elements cut out of varicolored cloth; designs depicted trees, animals, and, at times, even human figures. This adornment was common to both male and female costumes, especially in France where frivolities were readily adapted.

Women, from the descriptions of the poets, appeared as divine creatures, full of grace and beauty. But even then that beauty was not completely natural; the woman of the Fourteenth Century wisely corrected her own nature to harmonize it with the ideal proposed by the artists of her time. The poets of the *dolce stil novo,* inspired by Saint Francis and Saint Thomas, considered woman as an abstract incarnation of beauty, or as a symbol of purity, divine wisdom, and philosophy (Figure 143).

In this environment of peaceful beauty and platonic love, Dante's genius blossomed as, enamored of the ideal Beatrice, he contemplated man's moral philosophy. And it was his genius, passion, and fantasy that banished the darkness of the Middle Ages and specified the individual values of man.

Figure 143. Heinrich von Meissen, famous for his eulogies of the fair sex, is seen conducting his musicians. The fanciful costumes of the minstrels are noteworthy. Code from Universitätsbibliothek Heidelberg.

The Fourteenth Century   **147**

In the Fourteenth Century, the simple, long line of dresses was well studied to make the silhouette more slender; the less elaborate gowns were of a soft, golden cloth, the famous *panno d'oro,* which sometimes reflected a moon-silver light rather than gold. At times, on the simpler dresses was worn the *demi-ceint*—an elegant chain, loose on the hips, with hanging pendants in precious metals.

Women loved contrasts of colors and fabrics; and many costumes were accented by lining the long sleeves of the over-dress, or the ample cloaks, with different kinds of silk or velvet in dashing colors.

Colors were really new and refined: purple, hazel, cobalt blue, vermillion; silver gray velvet was embroidered with pearls. Gentle decorations were in fashion, full of movement, like flying birds or butterflies.

In all of Europe ladies' dresses found new accents of beauty; décolletages appeared deeper but a "modesty" patch, in Italy called *tassello,* almost always covered the cleavage. Women resembled angels in their long *cotardies* with wide, fluttering sleeves (Figure 144). The cotardie, as a style, originated in Italy, but it spread widely in France and later everywhere else. It was adopted by both men and women and consisted of an overdress, worn by women over a long white shirt, and by men over the short shirt which was inaugurated in that century. But so variously was it shaped that a single description would not be precise. In both the male and female version, however, the cotardie has tight-fitting undersleeves, very often with many little buttons.

The *truffeau* was a French hat made with a sort of elongated pack of false hair, which, when placed in gold nets embroidered with pearls, surrounded the head; noble ladies even set their crowns on it. The truffeaux had varied shapes, but always held a light veil attached (Figure 145).

Figure 144. *In this miniature showing a knight escorting his lady to a castle, we see the typical French* cotardie *with its fluttering outer sleeves. Louvre, Paris.*

Figure 145. A drawing derived from the Chroniques of Jean Froissart *which illustrates the meeting between Edward III and Philippa of Hainaut. Details of the Fourteenth Century feminine costume are apparent, particularly the distinctive hats: the* hennin *and the* truffeau. *The* tassello, *filling in the décolletages is quite apparent. By Gabrielli, author's collection.*

Figure 146. Miniature from La Cité des Dames *by Christine de Pisan. These ladies display the typical lines of fine feminine dress with cotardies and the coiffe with horns, called* cornettes. *Bibliothèque Nationale, Paris.*

The touret was a veil which passed under the chin, over the cheeks, and ended in a nice coiffe. It was to remain in style for two centuries and it can be seen exquisitely delineated at the beginning of the Sixteenth Century in some sketches and paintings by Albrecht Dürer.

Coiffes in white linen were commonly used; and sometimes they swept up at the sides in a graceful movement (Figure 146). The touret and the horned hat were worn also by ordinary women, who generally wore simple dresses with flat shoes in felt or rough clogs of wood.

The most original feminine hat was the *hennin*, which was created at the end of this century in Venice and took its name

History of Fashions

Figure 147. *A fresco by Simone Martini (c. 1283–1344) portraying Guidoriccio da Fogliano illustrates a fashionable indulgence of the Fourteenth Century: the rider and his horse are covered with elaborate cloaks of identical design and color. Palazzo Publico, Siena.*

Figure 148. *A medieval miniature showing Tristan and Isolde in conversation illustrates the costumes of the Trecento. Isolde, wearing a crown, has a dress of simple line, high waistline, and wide sleeves lined with fur. One of the ladies wears a coiffe of the cornette type. Tristan is clothed simply in a long zimarra. Bibliothèque Nationale, Paris.*

from Madame Hennin, who first wore it. It consisted of a long, rigid cone of silk or velvet, with a piece of voile or lace hanging from the point.

To enhance the beauty and richness of the headdresses, the hair was usually very simply arranged; divided at the forehead, and braided with red ribbons around the head.

In Fourteenth-Century clothing, color gives a striking note of life and gaiety, and particular attention is paid to its effects. The overdress of Guidoriccio da Fogliano, seen in the famous painting of Simone Martini, is in harmony with the horse's caparison and offers a very effective example of the importance of color and its bizarre disposition during this period (Figure 147).

With the passing of the years, elegance became richer, even if less fantastic. The celebrated cloaks of Gubbio were lined with gold or silver, or with vair. The Florentine textile workers imported raw silks from the Orient; and the famous dye workers treated it according to a special technique and then exported it. The silks thus were enriched in colors of delicate hues which even surpassed Oriental levels. Florentine ladies became the finest in all Europe, the most gracious and cultivated.

Poetry also entered the city of flowers (Figure 148). It was an exotic poetry, originating from Provence and composed of languid words and melancholic melodies. To it, the Tuscans joined their sense of joyfulness and their scholastic and metaphysical subtleties, derived from the University of Bologna where they studied Plato, Aristotle, and Thomas Aquinas. The dolce stil novo was the new expression of art which ended the Middle Ages.

Dante closed the Middle Ages and, foreseeing the future, initiated the new epoch that would be known as the Renaissance.

History of Fashions

The Fifteenth Century

While the last traces of the Gothic spirit still glittered from the beautiful French paintings of Jean Fouquet, the spark of the Renaissance marked a renewal of classic antiquity. It arrived through classic studies, which played a key role in the aspirations of the Fifteenth Century. The best minds strove to live in keeping with the principles of antiquity, and the works of great Latin writers again reaped popular success.

The great new artists likewise were inspired by the best examples of Greco–Roman art, and they painted and sculpted the most beautiful nudes of all time. To perfect their knowledge of the natural movements of the human body, they studied anatomy; but they also concerned themselves with man's expression. So deeply were they involved in this research that often one can see in their creations the effects of the artists' personal struggles.

Discovering human nature, the costume appeared liberated from officialdom; it was to develop with a new spirit of decoration. All the life of this century is reflected in the extraordinary flourishing of the arts and in the evolution of clothing

153

Figure 149. An Italian lady of 1400. She wears unusual gloves, elegantly lined; her dress is high-waisted with an overskirt draped in front and probably held in place by a troussoir. *The cloak, with the long, open sleeve is rather atypical of the time. Print from the Barberini Library, Rome.*

and its many accessories, whose production at times rose to the importance of full-fledged industries (Figure 149).

The large scenes and spatial compositions already created by Giotto became full of fine details in the hands of the new artists. Filippo Brunelleschi invented architectural perspective and erected the *palazzi* of Florence, which seem to fix the time and mark of the Florentine civilization. Sandro Botticelli, painter of line and grace in movement, created effortlessly— like new music—a perfect harmony between personages and their environments. In his art he also created a manner—a symbolic manner of painting—that persisted throughout the Renaissance, and even later (Figure 150).

Antonio Pisano, known as Pisanello, joined together precision of contour and perfect balance, as we can see in his portraits, which are also exquisite studies and paintings of costume. He was painter, sculptor, and also the first scholar and official designer of costume (Figure 151). With his poetic intuition and a pronounced temperament for reality mixed with fantasy, Pisanello left us many fine studies of flowers and birds; horses, monkeys, and dogs; and precious, fairy-like designs of feminine hairdos. He was a marvelous interpreter of the then-current, international trend in art, called *Gotico fiorito,* and managed to transform it in keeping with the principles of rhythm and equilibrium.

Italy, at that time, was divided into many little states, and other nations in Europe were being consolidated. While the rest of Europe still lived in the darkness of the Middle Ages, Italy had its moment of greatest artistic and cultural splendor. Its unification was to come much later, but the brilliance of its art was already a reality.

The patronage of artists flourished, books were printed and widely distributed to spread the new knowledge before which the whole world bowed.

Figure 150. *Detail from the famous fresco,* Le Prove di Mose *by Botticelli. Two young shepherdesses are wearing embroidered shirts and shawls; their hairdos appear artfully ingenuous. Vatican Museum, Rome.*

Figure 151. *Study of male costumes by Pisanello. These three magnificent and sumptuous costumes are decorated with rich furs and refined embroideries. The hats, too, are lavishly styled; the man on the right wears the* ghirlanda, *which in this century becomes a new type of headdress for men, made of gold and enameled flowers and leaves. British Museum, London.*

Figure 152. *Detail from famous tapestry,* La Dame à la Licorne. *The young maid-in-waiting, proffering a casket of jewels to her mistress, displays a very unusual hairdo seemingly inspired by the unicorn of mythology, a pure, white, one-horned animal that could be captured only by virgins. Musée de Cluny, Paris.*

Many new materials and textiles also were created at this time. Genoa became famous for its velvets, and Venice for its beads of glass, used in a new kind of embroidery. In the same period, tapestry making started; it was particularly a Flemish art, but it developed in France and also in Italy (Figure 152).

The feminine dress was marked by a high waistline. Women generally wore fitted, short bodices and ample skirts, pleated below the belt to accentuate the abdomen (Figure 153). The sleeves, varied in elaboration, were given importance and, at times, touched notes of splendor; rich in fantasy cuts and knots, they often allowed glimpses of white lace to show from the shirt beneath. Décolletages shed modesty, became wider and deeper, and often were inspired by the daring necklines of the old deities. Many great artists, especially Botticelli, Crivelli, and Paolo Veronese, have played with this classic taste in their paintings of women.

Figure 153. Game of Tarots, *a painting by the Maestro dei Giochi Borromeo. In these elegant and characteristic Italian costumes of the Fifteenth Century we observe that a belt marks the high waistline and gathers the fullness of the skirt to the front. The smart hat, the* balzo, *is seen on two of the ladies and interpreted as a hairdo by the third. The men's hats are also interesting. Casa Borromeo, Milan.*

The Fifteenth Century 157

The painting of the Fifteenth Century, of both secular and religious subjects, illustrates precisely the characteristics of the female carriage and the dresses, in all their sophisticated and fantastic elegance. In no other epoch can we see so large a variety of styles in dress, cloaks, and hairdos as we find in these paintings (Figure 154). Many of the garments were given names, especially in Italy, where refined people engaged in a sort of name-finding game, made much of originality, and talked a great deal about who had named what first.

In the frescoes of Piero della Francesca, many unusual styles appear: different hats and coiffes, varying arrangements of color, and designs of cloaks, such as the famous *giornea,* hanging from the ladies' shoulders.

The gold garb of the Fourteenth Century became completely embroidered, and the great court painters dwelt on the description of the designs. Domenico Ghirlandaio, for example, reported every detail of the dress, jewels, and hairdos of the noble ladies he painted (Figure 155).

In the painting:

ARS VTINAM MORES
ANIMVMQVE EFFINGERE
POSSES PVLCHRIOR IN TER
RIS NVLLA TABELLA FORET
·MCCCCLXXXVIII·

Figure 155. Portrait of Giovanna Tornabuoni *by Domenico Ghirlandaio (1449–1494) is a superb example of the restrained elegance of Florentine aristocrats; the hairdress, the carriage, and the sobriety of jewels attest to a refined taste. Quite evident here is the slashed and detached outer sleeve which allows the soft material underneath to peek through. By kind permission of Baron H. H. Thyssen-Bornemisza.*

Figure 156. *Detail from Botticelli's* Primavera *showing a fine example of fashionable Renaissance hairdressing, composed of postiches, jewels, and varied ornaments added to the real hair. Uffizi Gallery, Florence. (Far left.)*

Figure 157. Maria Magdalena *by Carlo Crivelli (1430–1495). The beautiful and sophisticated hairdo and the elegant costume are original with Crivelli and typical of the popular treatment of sacred subjects. Nevertheless, the dress, preciously embroidered in gold, reflects some of the fashion peculiarities of the Fifteenth Century with the slashed sleeves and the high waistline. Rijksmuseum, Amsterdam. (Left.)*

Figure 158. *Detail from* Adoration of the Magi *by Gentile da Fabriano (c. 1360–1427). The two headdresses were inspired by the turbans used by Hebrew women. This painting is typical of the many Renaissance portrayals of biblical subjects in which ancient costumes were interpreted in the taste of the times. Uffizi Gallery, Florence. (Below.)*

Figure 159. Study for a fresco in St. Anastasia, Verona by Pisanello. These designs reveal an intense research for unusual hairdressings. Very clearly shown here is the custom of that time of shaving the forehead.

The most beautiful hairstyles were sophisticated symphonies of pearls, postiches, light feathers, ribbons, and jewels, minutely designed with imagination and realized with unbelievable skill (Figure 156).

Biblical paintings no longer inspired a sense of religion. Crivelli dressed his saints like courtesans (Figure 157). And some elegant madonnas, radiantly youthful and beautiful, who so sensually offer the breast to the Infant from the ingenious cuts concealed by the folds of the bodice, appear as extraordinarily earthly creatures. Thus they seem to reveal only the secrets of fashion and confirm the strong interest of Renaissance people in problems of esthetics and costume (Figure 158).

Women wore massive crowns decorated with leaves and flowers in enameled gold, or peacock feathers, called *garlands;* from these originated the *balzo,* the most beautiful hat and hairdo of this century. The balzo was a typically Italian hat, elegantly rounded, made of pearls, tiny feathers, little flowers, or enormous braids, and always very refined. It was placed on the head so as to leave free the high, shaved forehead (Figure 159). The slender neck then acquired an endless grace and appeared to be a fragile stem rising from the simple neckline, lowered at the nape of the neck.

Shoes were still pointed and always embroidered in velvet, satin, or light leather. Sometimes they were merely elegant stockings with stuffed points at the toe.

In Europe during the Fifteenth Century, costumes were sumptuous and diverse; and the most original fashions were rapidly transmitted from one country to another. From Italy and France came the most far-reaching influences, and from that time onward, France has demonstrated an unusual sense of and care for elegance. In Italy, at refined courts, the cos-

History of Fashions

tume was enriched and showed a great beauty of line and color, and a magnificence of fabrics (Figure 160). *Taffetas* was the newest fabric; it was rigid but also light as a feather, and it rustled like the wind among ferns.

Figure 160. *The frontal piece of a bridal chest illustrating the wedding of Boccaccio Adimari and Lisa Ricasoli by Maestro di Fucecchio. The sumptuous costumes of Tuscan nobility are beautifully illustrated: the ladies have embroidered gowns with trains, beautiful headdresses, and even a broadbrimmed hat made of peacock feathers; the gentlemen wear hats of velvet or fur and the softly draped chaperon. Their tunics and cloaks reveal the finest and most varied lines, while their assymetrical hosiery-shoes are remarkable in their highly contrasting designs. Galleria dell'Accademia, Florence.*

Figure 161. *Two statuettes from a famous fireplace of Dam, Netherlands. The sculptures were created in the Fifteenth Century and faithfully reflect the styles of that epoch. The first (a) shows a typical cloak and highwaisted dress, but the collar is unusual; a decorated balzo is worn with a cloth softly draped under the chin. The second figure (b) wears a typical truffeau with* bourrelet *and pendant veils. Rijksmuseum, Amsterdam.*

Figure 162. *Male figures from the fireplace of Dam showing three different ensembles of coats, hats, and decorated belts. The dagged sleeves of the first and third coats (a and c) are typically French. The richly draped hat trimmed with merlons (c) is a classic chaperon.*

Figure 163. *Detail from the* Corteggio dei Re Magi *by Benozzo Gozzoli. One of the kings wears a sumptuous costume of green brocade, embroidered in gold, and bordered with mink. The unusual crown of gold spikes encrusted with jewels rests on a broad, soft hat. Chapel of Palazzo Medici-Riccardi, Florence.*

Figure 164. Un Miracolo di San Bernardino *by Fiorenzo di Lorenzo (1440–1522). Details of various costumes of gentlemen and pages can be seen in this street battle. Pinacoteca, Perugia. Foto Alinari.*

Because of these strong influences, the styles were more varied, but fashion from one country to the next was, consequently, less individualistic (Figures 161, 162).

The dress of both men and women often was decorated with fur, primarily ermine, sable, and fox tails. Sometimes the natural motifs of furs were repeated in the embroidered linings. Ladies having a train used a new jewel to hold it. Artistically wrought, it was called a *troussoir*. In contrast, ordinary women still retained fustian and woolen cloth, and the line of their dress remained almost monastic.

The male costume was very refined and capricious (Figure 163). Men loved color and originality; some nobles particularly preferred one special color. Their stockings were also in vivid colors and sometimes vertically striped (Figure 164).

The Fifteenth Century 165

Figure 165. *Detail from the* Arrival of the English Ambassadors, *one of a series of paintings portraying the Legend of St. Ursula, by Vittore Carpaccio (c. 1455–1526). The figure second from right wears a close-fitting doublet, laced across the front, with fashionable slashed sleeves; he also wears a purse hanging from his belt. He and the gentlemen on the left with the ample, knee-length coat wear small, round-crowned hats. Academy of Fine Arts, Venice.*

Because of the high regard in which all the elite of this interesting epoch held the costume, the profession of costume designer was a natural development; and it was he who created the line, the significance, the contrast of colors, and their assortment and symphony. Many great artists of this period were scholars of costume; among them, Pisanello, Holbein, and even Leonardo da Vinci.

Carpaccio introduced Venice to the Renaissance, and, together with the silent canals and architectural details which

History of Fashions

Figure 167. *Detail from the* Game of the Palm *by Maestro di Giochi Borromeo. In this scene of a typical social pastime we have an outstanding example of the* robe à la française *which combined elements of French and Italian fashions. By kind permission of the Prince Borromeo.*

he liked to illustrate faithfully, he described some particular costumes and unusual hairdos and hats (Figures 165, 166). In one instance, he shows some Venetian ladies seated on the terrace, drying their hair in the sun—hair dyed "venetian blond" with the help of gold powder and carrot extract. This is a *mise en scene* which is not conventional and not in keeping with the elegance of the period. However, it clearly describes and underlines an interesting practice.

The "Maestro di Giochi," Borromeo, in his fine paintings full of elegant people, depicts especially well the court life and the varied games they played at that time; for example, the "play of the palm" and the game of the *Tarocchi,* played with tarot cards at tables (Figure 167; see also Figure 153).

Sometimes it is also possible to see in those paintings feminine images revealing different fashions in the same costume. This development occurred chiefly at the beginning of the Fifteenth Century when the personal taste and intelligence of Valentina Visconti, Duchess of Orléans at the court of France,

The Fifteenth Century

a

b

Figure 168. (a) *Detail from the* Story of the Holy Cross *by Piero della Francesco (c. 1420–1492). The Queen of Sheba greets King Solomon who wears an extraordinary, sumptuous cloak. The ladies-in-waiting have interesting coiffes and headdressings. Various styles of headgear are shown by the men. (b) Another detail shows the kneeling Queen of Sheba and her maidens wearing fine cloaks and coiffes of varied designs. In the foreground is the cloak-cape called the* giornea; *made of velvet and lined in silk, it is finished with a border of jagged tongues. (c) Detail showing the simple headdressing and delicate crown worn by the Queen of Sheba. Church of San Francesco, Arezzo.*

c

Figure 169. Portrait of a noblewoman by Antonio Pollaiuolo (1432–1498). Many particulars of a fine hairdressing, jewels, and embroidery are shown in this painting. Museo Poldi-Pezzoli, Milan.

was surpassed by Diane de Poitiers, who spread the refinements of the court of Paris throughout Lombardy. As a result, some imitations of French fashions were mixed with Italian styles; and we can see in Figure 167, for example, the high belted dress, *all'italiana,* worn with the balzo, while the sleeves are outlined with long tongues, *à la française.*

In the great feasts of the Renaissance, the most elegant costume assured the success not only of the gentleman wearing it, but also of the artist who designed it (Figure 168). These celebrated artists also created the costumes for the literary theater, where actors wore the dress of the epoch for modern dramatic plays, and historical Greco–Roman costumes for representations of the stories, tragedies, and comedies of antiquity. The literary theater of the Renaissance was laic and represented the revival of man's individualism—a new man, striving for perfection in his personality and liberty, and seeking to become what Montaigne would call, "a man of singular spirit and highest rank. . . ."

The heroes of the Renaissance did not seek to be just good citizens; rather, they wanted very much to be the "universal man." This goal appeared evident in the language, the mentality, and the common tendency of the theater. The "universal man" became the secret and sense of all human effort, and of the intellectual movement known as "humanism" (Figure 169).

It was not yet the time of conflicts between faith and reason, but pagan beauty had confronted the Christian religion in the conscience of the artists. Two opposite worlds collided and mingled. The genius of the greatest artists probably reconciled the dissensions, for they looked to Greek antiquity with eyes made tender by the religion of Christ, and to Christianity with eyes blinded by the splendor of the Greek civilization. And so, the new world of the Italian Renaissance was generated.

The Sixteenth Century

The Renaissance, because it opposed the mortifying doctrines of the Middle Ages, gave man a great sense of faith. The very word "Renaissance" was fashioned from this kind of new faith in man's ability to be creative in the arts and the sciences. It was a sort of resurrection of other great epochs, enriched now by new conquests of man's genius.

In the Sixteenth Century, Rome became the artistic and universal capital. Bramante created in architecture the new physiognomy of Rome; and Michelangelo composed the strength of its aspect in the rhythm of majestic and regular proportions. The greatest monumental sculptor of his time, perhaps of all ages, Michelangelo introduced the spirit of compassion to modern sculpture.

Leonardo da Vinci softened the shadows and diffused the light to give figures and landscapes a legendary quality (Figure 170). He tried by science and intuition to understand and conquer nature. Leonardo, instigator of a pictorial school, invented a new theory of color; he was expert in anatomy, physics, and engineering; he knew the laws of perspective and

Figure 170. Portrait of a Lady with Ermine *by Leonardo da Vinci (1452–1519). Observing the sober elegance of this costume and hairdo, we realize that even Leonardo was conscious of costume design. The front of the lady's hair is smoothly drawn over the ears and passed under the chin; a transparent veil covers the forehead and is held in place by the* ferronière. *Czartoriski Museum, Cracow.*

wrote treatises of painting. In fact, with his myriad skills and his humanistic spirit, he typifies, more than anyone else, the "Renaissance Man."

Raphael completed the fusion of two worlds through beauty; his art united Christian principles and the "school of Athens." He described the environment of courts, the cultivated and aristocratic society; evading political strifes, he sought perfection of forms with the elegance of a fine conversation.

Raphael did not greatly admire jewels and wealthy ladies, and so he painted sumptuous portraits only when they were especially commissioned. Frequently he sought to reveal by the facial expression the spirit of the Renaissance, preferring,

The Sixteenth Century 173

then, to paint simple, unadorned people. A beautiful portrait of an unknown woman with her hands crossed and wearing a simple, sober, dark-colored costume, catches our interest by its mysterious expression (Figure 171).

Titian solved the problem of light in a completely new way, and all his images seem as if they were seen in the sun, softened by orange and gold and red light. He was a most celebrated painter especially because of his particular personality, both dignified and profound, and his particular sense of color. These qualities we can see in his famous portraits (Plate 7). Never did he seek to adulate his important models; rather, he tried always to find the best in their expressions. All the most powerful rulers of Europe availed themselves of his art: Charles V of Spain, Francis I of France, and Pope Paul III. Titian's color always projects an extraordinary splendor; a warm tone of gold illuminates his nudes. He created at that time a special "Titianesque" type of feminine beauty.

Renaissance women were distinguished not only for their beauty, but also for their special qualities of education, culture, and taste in costume. The great artists created a feminine esthetic ideal; and, as in other ages, women strove to correct their natural physical shortcomings in order to achieve the esthetic ideal of their epoch. They did not care for the costume simply for the love of fashions; rather, they sought to find a personality in the costume. With the aim of confirming their special character and level in society, they developed a thirst for knowledge and culture and were fascinated by the classic Greek and Roman arts. They were remarkably intelligent and erudite and were ready to discuss the most serious cultural problems; some of them devoted their energies to government and, sometimes, even defended their country with armor and arms—just like men. Indeed, there flourished superior types of women in every field.

Figure 171. The Lady in Green by
Raphael (1483–1520) illustrates this
great artist's powers of characterization.
The simple costume in olive greens high-
lighted with lacquer-red velvet echos the
sober dignity of this woman. Palazzo
Ducale, Urbino.

Figure 172. *Detail from a painting by Bonifacio Veronese (1487–1553) showing an extraordinary headdressing in gold and pearls with a jeweled pendant. Academy of Fine Arts, Venice.*

Figure 173. Portrait of a Lady *by Paolo Veronese (1528–1588). This painting illustrates many of the precious fabrics used during the Renaissance. The sumptuous velvet dress is partially covered by a transparent cloak of delicate Venetian lace which seems to be fastened to the shoulders with heavy golden ornaments. A gold belt with an elaborate buckle outlines the pointed bodice. And the magnificent sleeves are made of the famous* découpé *velvet over a golden ground. Louvre, Paris.*

In the Sixteenth Century, costume also became freed from the chains of tradition; and everyone, man and woman, chose his personal manner of dressing according to his own taste and fantasy. High society prepared fabulous feasts where beautiful women showed truly magnificent hairstyles, such as the famous *en tête,* composed of feathers and jewels (Figure 172).

Venice, a powerful commercial center, did not concern itself with the literature and philosophy of Florence, nor with the arts of architecture and sculpture so nobly developed in Rome. Instead, there arose an outstanding school of painting in which color was the most striking characteristic. The artists depicted the gaiety and the intellectual refinements of that most unusual city. The embellishment of costume and palazzi became a major endeavor.

Paolo Veronese was one of the most important Venetian masters of painting of this century, and he was also a painter of costume. In many portraits he depicted elongated bodices, transparent cloaks and veils, and gold-embroidered sleeves with cuffs of Venetian lace (Figure 173).

In Venice a special lace was created, so beautiful that sometimes it became an inspiration even to poets and painters. In 1457, the Duchess Giovanna Dandolo had recognized the full importance of that craft, and the little island of Burano became famous. Then, in 1595, the Duchess Morosina Morosini assembled and organized 130 women workers in a factory to make exquisite embroideries in lace under the direction of Catina Gardin, who was an artisan and an artist of creative imagination.

One of the first designers of sets for the theater, employed mainly at the Austrian court, was the Italian Giuseppe Arcimboldi. He worked at organizing parties, tournaments, masquerades, feasts; and he became famous more for his spirited inventions than for a profound personal value. He created fantastic allegories of the seasons, in which human

Figure 174. La Bella Simonetta *by Piero di Cosimo (1462–1521) displays an intricate headdress of multiple braids interlaced with strings of pearls and pendant stones. Musée Condé, Chantilly.*

figures were represented by capricious combinations of vegetable elements. Moreover, throughout the Renaissance period it was the fashion to compose the human image with Greek motifs and decorative elements like fruits, flowers, and leaves. Among those working in this style were Botticelli, Crivelli, and Veronese.

Besides pure art, of which they have remained among the greatest masters, many of these artists liked to engage in some applied arts such as jewelry and fabric design for the aristocracy. Many European painters dedicated their art to costume design, with all its accessories, and the elaboration of hairdos (Figure 174).

While Italy dominated the world of art, the power of Charles V grew and, after the discovery of America, Spanish influence spread throughout Europe. As a result, that influence appeared in costume, also, and introduced strange fashion variations: pleats became heavy; diamonds, rubies, and emeralds were used lavishly; and earrings, diadems, and necklaces began to oppress the silhouette. The ruff imprisoned the fine necks and made rigid and dramatic both expression and carriage (Figures 175, 176).

History of Fashions

Figure 176. *Caterina de' Medici, widow of Henry II, in mourning costume. After two centuries of being white, the mourning costume for regal widows is now black. The heavily pleated skirt is attached to a fitted, pointed bodice worn over an iron corset which determined the rigid carriage typical of this age. The widow's coiffe is the* conque, *supported by iron wires; her ruff, cuffs, and gloves are white. From "Le Costume Civil en France" Flammarion, Paris.*

Figure 175. Portrait of Eleonora di Toledo *by Agnolo Bronzino (1502–1572) shows a sumptuous costume of découpé velvet. The nets interlaced with pearls which cover the shoulders and her simply arranged hair are typically Spanish. Uffizi Gallery, Florence.*

The Sixteenth Century

Figure 177. Portrait of Laudomia de' Medici *by Agnolo Bronzino (1502-1572). The aristocratic dress of black velvet and the little bonnet are richly embroidered with pearls. Here we see that in Italy the Spanish ruff was used with much sobriety and the fan-like type was preferred. Uffizi Gallery, Florence.*

Gold thread was woven on dark backgrounds of silk; the deep décolletages of the free Italian Renaissance were only indicated to give a line to the dress, for the bodice actually was closed to the neck (Figure 177). There was a rich splendor of fabrics, embroideries, and jewels, but the special characteristic of the feminine costume was the rigidity given to it by the iron corsets and stiff ruffs; these were widely used because custom made them mandatory for both men and women. In fact, because Spanish custom preserved many of the medieval principles and did not allow the freedom so characteristic of Renaissance custom and costume—extraordinarily modern in its conception—it chose to ignore the grace of that style.

In the Sixteenth Century Albrecht Dürer, a German artist, was the most prominent representative of graphic design in the sense that he used color as secondary in importance to the design itself (Figure 178). He was concerned about the proportions of the human body and was inspired by Italian theories of drawing and perspective. His woodcuts and engravings, as well as his paintings, established him as the leading master of the German school, second only to Italy in artistic importance in that age (Figure 179).

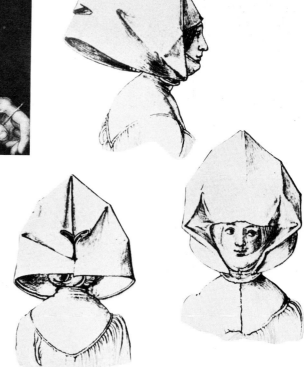

Figure 179. *Interesting costume studies by Dürer: characteristics of the coiffe known as the* touret *are very clearly illustrated. British Museum, London.*

· ANNO · ÆTATIS · SVÆ · XLIX ·

Figure 180. Portrait of Henry VIII by Hans Holbein (1497–1543). The King's richly embroidered velvet doublet is made lighter by perforations filled with puffed out silk. Galleria Nazionale, Rome; Alinari-Art Reference Bureau.

Figure 181. German Gunmaster. The costume of this military man—broad-brimmed hat covered with panaches, fashionably slashed sleeves, and knee breeches under the suit of armor—denotes a position of high rank and esteem. Henry E. Huntington Library, San Marino, California.

Plate 1. Goat of Ur, *an offering stand made of gold, silver, and lapis lazuli over a wooden core; it is a remarkable creation from c. 6000 years ago. Symbolizing fertility, the powerful beast stands among branching plants. British Museum, London. (Left.)*

Plate 2. *This head of a vulture made of glass is a gem created during the Achaemenid period of Persian history (600–330 B.C.). British Museum, London. (Above.)*

Plate 3. *Pectorals and earrings in gold and precious stones from Tutankhamen's treasury. Cairo Museum. (Below.)*

Plate 4. Fresco from a tomb of Ruvo shows women rhythmically dancing in a funeral procession. National Museum, Naples.

Plate 5. Roman fresco from Stabiae presents a delightful personification of Spring. National Museum, Naples.

Plate 6. Empress Theodora and Her Retinue, *one of the remarkable mosaics created in Ravenna during the Sixth Century* A.D. *San Vitale, Ravenna; Art Reference Bureau.*

Plate 7. Portrait of a Man *by Titian (1477–1576).*
Reproduced by Courtesy of the Trustees of the National
Gallery, London.

Plate 8. *Four models of elaborate Eighteenth Century French hairstyles by Depain. Carnavalet Museum, Paris.*

Plate 9. Mademoiselle Rivière *by Jean Auguste Dominique Ingres (1780–1867). Louvre, Paris; Art Reference Bureau.*

Plate 10. The Market *by Paul Gauguin (1848–1903). Kunstmuseum, Basel.*

Plate 11. (*Above*) *By Rosana Pistolese.*
Plate 12. (*Below*) *By Ken Scott.*
Plate 13. (*Right*) *By Giuseppe Picone.*
Contemporary textile designs produced by artists in Italy for High Fashion. *Courtesy of the artists.*

Plate 14. *An asymmetric costume created and hand printed by Livio de Simone of Capri. Courtesy of the artist. Photo: Corrado di Villermosa.*

Plate 15. *Enormous* paenula *of black cotton printed with stylized leaves by Livio de Simone. Courtesy of the artist. Photo: Corrado di Villermosa.*

Hans Holbein, another great German painter of that period, is famous for his portraits, especially those he did in England at the court of Henry VIII (Figure 180). His art is a wonderful example of Italian influence—everywhere prevalent—combined with German brilliance of draftsmanship.

The fashion of portraits in the time of the Renaissance arose chiefly from the affluence of the aristocracy and the merchants (Figure 181); but sometimes the great artists also had the good fortune of meeting splendid "professional" models, interesting and well dressed as people of that epoch generally were.

Very often, in the portraits, the feminine costumes show wonderful Tuscan fabrics in velvet relief on a background of satin, all in fantastic colors. The sleeves usually are made with large strips, fixed at several points by little rose-shaped buckles or little wheels for buttons. Strings of pearls encircle the neck and fall on the breast; belts in gold and precious stones mark the waistline.

Characteristic for men were the balloon-shaped breeches with long, vertical slashes worn with a close-fitting doublet (Figure 182). Noblemen preferred short cloaks of embroidered velvet; or, over embroidered costumes, they wore simple cloaks in dark velvet with large lapels, very often in fur, with two slashes for the arms.

Both men and women wore the soft, little hat in velvet, trimmed with feathers and called the *toque*. Of Spanish origin, it later became particularly smart and varied. The fantastic hairstyles of the past were now replaced by turbans, veils tied under the chin, or little cowls shaped with iron wires.

The Sixteenth Century
183

Figure 182. Portrait of Henry II *of France illustrates the classic men's costume of the Sixteenth Century: long belted doublet with* basques, *vertically decorated; embroidered shirt; and striped balloon breeches. The hat, a* toque *with a small feather, is also typical. Musée Condé, Chantilly.*

Figure 183. Portrait of Charles IX *of France by François Clouet (1522–1572). This costume is again typical of this century, but carried out with a slightly more exaggerated taste: the balloon breeches are fuller, the waist is cinched more tightly, and the smooth, rounded line of waistcoat was achieved by lining it with cardboard. Clearly shown are the shoes with slashes on top called* en pied d'ours; *a short cloak and the toque complete the costume. Louvre, Paris.*

The shoes of the Sixteenth Century introduced a new style. They were still flat but were made with a differently shaped, triangular sole. This shoe was called *en pied d'ours,* and real or embroidered slashes on the vamp often emphasized that style resembling a bear's paw (Figure 183).

A special waistcoat, called *panseron,* came into fashion in France at the end of the Sixteenth Century. Stiffly lined with common, gray cardboard, it was abnormally distended and displayed a sort of rigid, false stomach. It was worn over non-matching breeches that reached to the knee. It should be pointed out, however, that it was a rather short-lived *bizarrerie* of style, which appeared often among the costumes of the French version of the *Commedia dell'Arte.*

All is full of contrasts and life in the paintings of this period: all images, male and female, show a temperament, a taste, as well as a class difference. At times we also find beautiful women, young and simple, not noble but not yet courtesans, who display a sort of mixed elegance of fashionable sleeves or gloves, and then indicate their social status by some modest detail. To complete their costumes, men wore necklaces and rings, buckles and buttons, and even diadems and fancy hair-dos.

In France and Italy there were many tailors. In the retinue of each important and rich personage of the Renaissance was the private tailor. And artists often painted their portraits, sometimes in exchange for some personal clothing or as a reward for the intelligent regard and artistic care they gave to the cut and proportions.

Interesting, too, are the costumes of the servants who appear in many paintings (Figure 184). They were created for dramatic effect and consisted of asymmetric breeches, stockings held up by garters, and shoes of decorated felt or leather. Little Negro pages were in fashion at that time; young Africans or

History of Fashions

Turks were brought to Venice and used as gondoliers or as watchmen for the palaces and ships in the lagoons. Some even worked as confectioners and perfumers.

The refinement of the Italian courts (where elegance actually established the foundations of the "line" of future fashions), the original French taste, and the spreading influence of powerful Spain acted in concert so that throughout Europe, as well as in England, the costume, generally speaking, became very similar (Figure 185). If we look at the details, we do observe that the Spanish costume was richer, more heavily embroidered, and more dramatic in color; the German quasi-monastic feminine costume seemed to be in contrast with masculine styles, which were surprising for their merry bells and ribbons. Everywhere, however, the Renaissance costume

The Sixteenth Century 185

Figure 186. *From* Esther in the Presence of Assuerus *by Paolo Veronese. This detail shows three young ladies in splendid costumes typical of the Italian Renaissance. The hairstyling exemplifies the Grecism of this period. Uffizi Gallery, Florence.*

Figure 187. Jewels attributed to Benvenuto Cellini illustrate the great artistic merit of Italian goldworking in the Sixteenth Century. These imaginative creations are made of gold, enamel, and irregular pearls—the so-called barocco *pearls,* which inspired many artists and gave their name to the artistic style and taste of the Seventeenth Century. Museo degli Argenti, Florence.

was exuberant and, at the same time, studied to produce precise effects. In the Italian taste, the effects were directed by and contained in the spirit of the classical, which nevertheless produced surprising theatrical effects in life as well as on the stage (Figure 186).

It was at the time of Benvenuto Cellini that ladies of the various courts had superb jewels (Figure 187). From the second half of the Fifteenth Century, when Lorenzo the Magnificent was famous for his splendid jewels which he ordered from the same great artists whom he protected, and through all of the Sixteenth Century it was the fashion for men also to wear elegant chains and necklaces. Goldsmiths and jewelers created large and long collars, filigreed, granulated, and engraved; some collars were made of gold chains studded with gems or enriched with a precious pendant. Some of these chains had a special story, either political or amorous, describing an event

The Sixteenth Century

or a personal characteristic of the wearer—as, for example, one made of little tongues that Francis I of France gave to Pietro Aretino as a symbol of admiration for his eloquence, but also as a memento of the virulence of Aretino's criticism and writing.

With the prevailing humanistic spirit of the Sixteenth Century, the costumes became more intensively representative of the individual and of society, of man in the Renaissance and of the new society that stemmed from the Renaissance (Figure 188).

Meanwhile, challenging the excessive intellectualism of the literary theater (of which we spoke in the preceding chapter), there originated the theater of the comics, which parodied the court theaters but remained quite unknown until men of letters felt its value and strength. It was the Commedia dell'Arte which used a new expressionistic language made of gestures and tones. In this kind of theater the costume became symbolic and thereby determined the triumph of the mask. There followed a rich flow of new masks: tragic, comic, grotesque types; good and evil masks, representing human attitudes and characters. There were many affinities between the popular theater of antiquity and the Commedia dell'Arte. It is very important to note in that phenomenon the repetition of necessary forms, created by similar social situations which inevitably inspire comic invention and create tradition. The Sixteenth Century was the natural time to renew as an actuality the classical theater, which until then had been limited to experimental, intellectualistic interpretation.

During the second half of this century in England, while some of the highest personalities of the court, illustrious men and priests, were condemned to execution, and Sir Thomas More, Anne Boleyn, Mary Stuart, and many others were going to the gallows, the English theater came into existence

Figure 188. Portrait of Veronica Gambara *by Il Correggio (1494–1534). Stylistically, this artist, only a few years younger than Raphael, presages the trends of Baroque art. Here, in a beautiful painting of light and shadow, he presents a very personal interpretation of costume and hairdo. The Hermitage, Leningrad.*

The Sixteenth Century

and evolved in a special climate of ghosts. It appeared between the Renaissance and Baroque ages and evidenced a sort of hybridism—a strange combination of the medieval, popular spectacle mixed with some spirit of the Renaissance theater; and it remained like that until the time of the Restoration. In order to understand the form that this theater assumed, it is necessary to establish an emotive rapport between it and its historical epoch, and thus we refer to it as the "Elizabethan Theater."

The first public theater was constructed in wood in 1574 by James Burbage in London on the right bank of the Thames. It was called simply "The Theatre." While the Commedia dell'Arte in Italy had brought women to the stage (who, incidentally, achieved instant success with the audience), in England at this time and even during the Seventeenth Century the feminine roles were still played by men. Actors and authors were poorly paid, and often both arts were practiced by one man. Also, it was convenient for them to be engaged by important gentlemen of the court because the patrons' names protected both the actors and the company.

William Shakespeare, born in Stratford on Avon in 1574, began as actor and author. His company gradually moved from the patronage of titled men to that of the Lord Chamberlain, and later assumed the name of "The King's Men" under James I. Shakespeare knew Latin and French, and he was able to read Italian poetry. He can be considered the greatest dramatic author after the extraordinary flourishing of the classic Greeks. His contemporaries adored him, the Eighteenth Century rejected him, and the Nineteenth Century exalted him. An artist of immense talent, he led the life of a normal man with all the ordinary tribulations. But so powerful is the influence of art, the world ignores the man and sees only the artist in the light of his great work.

The Seventeenth Century

From the extraordinary shapes of the pearls which Benvenuto Cellini and other great jewelers of the Sixteenth Century framed with gold and precious stones, *Barocco* (or Baroque style) takes its name. A new force, the Baroque style developed in Rome, far from classic tradition and proportions. Baroque is a representation of the "bizarre" and, in a way, its refinement and exaggeration. Rome, artistic capital of architecture and painting, saw the rise and spread of an anti-Roman, anticlassic art, which marked the triumph of fantasy and color.

In painting and sculpture Baroque generally is characterized by a preference for the picturesque and the superlative; perhaps it lacks the deeper conviction of classic art, but this void is masked by the exaggerations and accentuations of movement. To emphasize an absolute freedom of form, it sought very strong modes of expression.

For all artists, in all countries, Lorenzo Bernini has been a great source of inspiration. He was the master who dressed Rome with precious marble swags, bas-reliefs, and twisted columns decorated with garlands of flowers and small *putti*

Figure 189. Self Portrait *by Lavinia Fontana (1552–1602) shows an example of the Italian embroidery made with glass beads from Venice; the fan-shaped collar is of Venetian lace. Accademia di San Luca, Rome.*

(winged golden cherubs) suspended on merry festoons—all seemingly seeking the development and elaboration of fine motifs from the Sixteenth Century.

The Renaissance had been, in itself, the greatest innovation of civilization; so full of ideas, new life, and customs, it seems that it must have lasted for a long, long time. Nonetheless, the Seventeenth Century managed to appear new.

Bernini also accomplished the construction of large theaters, and, consequently, stage productions were modified. Space became enormous, and actors seemed to grow gigantic as they came closer to the audience. And with the scenographic triumph was born the melodrama, the music drama which tried to unite the ancient and the modern theater by using a unique universal language of joy and sorrow. Claudio Monteverdi (1564–1643), mandola player at the Gonzaga Court, broke the chains of convention and renewed contact with the popular sensitivity.

The Baroque theatrical costume was not tied precisely to the text, but sometimes appeared as a separate and suggestive motif in the spectacle. This was, in fact, the happiest period for the *Intermezzo,* for allegories, and for special effects. In the Renaissance theater, the "Interval" had been closely linked to the development of erudite comedy and had cultural and literary character. Now, on the contrary, it seemed to be an isolated representation whose sole purpose was to create surprise. The costume, therefore, appeared as the free expression of an extemporaneous inspiration.

The tournament, evolving from its previous feudal forms, came to have a purely spectacular function and demonstrated the need for panoramic and choreographic effects. Played in the theater, the tournament became a performance; with jousters as actors, and uniforms as costumes.

French drama, which had roamed from one court to another during the Sixteenth Century, was finally given its first stable theater at the start of the Seventeenth Century. It was called the "Théâtre de Marais" and was located in the Hôtel de Bourgogne in Paris.

Through the Commedia dell'Arte, most parts of the Renaissance theater, both literary and popular, survived to stimulate the theaters of other countries. Shakespeare, Calderón, Molière, Marivaux, Lope de Vega—all reveal some heritages of the comedy of art. Lope de Vega, the great founder of the Spanish theater, effectively illustrated all the aspects of the Spain of his time in his numberless productions of historical, psychological, and costume dramas.

French fashion attempted to free itself from Spanish influence and succeeded to such a degree that even the favorites of the king of Spain chose the grace and fantasy of French styles.

Spanish influence, however, was prolonged in Italy because Spain then dominated the more important Italian regions of Lombardy and the Kingdom of Naples (Figure 189). The first to divorce itself from Spanish taste was Genoa; because of intensive commerce between the two countries, the splendid black velvet of Genoa, from the work shops of Zoagli and Chiavari, found its way into Spain and was used even in the Spanish court (Figure 190).

The Seventeenth Century   **193**

Figure 190. Portrait of a Lady *by Leandro Bassano (1557–1622). The string of large pearls worn by this plump lady is a typical accessory of the Seventeenth Century. Her singular hairdo is reminiscent of the mythological* en corymbe *style of antiquity. The prosperous décolletage of the black velvet dress is graced by a ruffled* lattuga *collar. Museo di Capodimonte, Naples.*

Figure 191. Portrait of Marguerite of Austria, *wife of Phillipe III of Spain by Pantoja de la Cruz (1549–1608). The Queen wears an elaborate costume, stiffly embroidered on silk; it is enriched with starched lace cuffs and ruff and a lavish display of gems. Prado Museum, Madrid.*

History of Fashions

When Ferdinando I de' Medici consented to the marriage of his niece, Maria, to Henry IV, King of France, he had in mind the renewal of trade between Florence and Paris. And the elegant level of life in both capitals was to prove a guaranty for the successful outcome of the motives behind the royal marriage. Maria de' Medici, not in her first years as a queen, but later when she was forced to give up her political role (like the majority of other Italian princesses), took a great interest in clothing elegance. And from that moment, France and Italy were able to free themselves from Spanish supremacy in styles.

The harmonious beauty which the Renaissance glorified was concealed, at the beginning of this century, and contained in the geometric rigidity apparent in Spanish portraits. But soon the costume began to change frequently and spawned many styles. Now, with the help of paintings and portraits, we will attempt to place them in their individual periods.

In the first period, until about 1610, there were many remnants of the Sixteenth Century for both men and women: for example, the ruff and the rigid bodice, pointed in front and ending in the brief basque (Figure 191). On the ruff, the face seemed to be placed as on a tray of white lace; and the woman's small head was pyramid shaped, with a triumph of little fruits, flowers, and bells creating the hairdo. To this little confection short aigrettes were often added.

The game of tennis came into fashion but was played only by men. The *pavane,* a Spanish dance which emulated the gracious and proud movements of the peacock, was danced at the court. The "Tour d'Argent" (still a celebrated restaurant in Paris) then became famous because there, for the first time, forks were put at the disposal of the guests. It was a time of elegance!

The Seventeenth Century   **195**

Figure 192. *French and Swedish costumes, c. 1630. Upper left (a) is the Earl of Noailles with a huge rabat and feathered hat topping his costume. At his right (b) shows Henry of Lorraine, Duke of Guise, wearing an unusual wig ending in a beribboned braid on his left shoulder. Next (c) represents Gustavus Adolphus, King of Sweden, wearing a sober costume; the black and white, the general lines, the natural hair, and pointed beard all recall the fashions of the Sixteenth Century. Far right (d) the Duke of Orleans displays an original and atypical costume. Leloir, "Histoire du Costume," Ernst (Publisher), Paris.*

Figure 193. *Portrait of a Woman by Nicholas Elias, c. 1620, reveals the refined and personal accents of Dutch fashions to which the splendid laces always add a special grace. Leloir, "Histoire du Costume," Ernst, Paris.*

Figure 194. Dutch Children *by A. Cuyp, c. 1620, show how closely the children's fashions echo the styles of their elders. Leloir, "Histoire du Costume," Ernst, Paris.*

Men and women wore jackets with basques cut in many trapezoidal pieces; the embroidery for both was made of gold in vertical braids (Figure 192). Because sleeves were closely fitted to the arms, independent of the dress, and tied to the body with ribbons under the jackets, the arm hole was reinforced with a padded border of cloth, called *bouillonné.*

A special hoop skirt called *vertugadin* determined the line of women's skirts (Figures 193, 194). The first type was the *vertugadin à tambour,* which enlarged the hips approximately twelve inches on each side (Figure 195). The term "vertugadin," making a very French pun, meant "guardian of virtue."

Figure 195. *A German woman portrayed by W. Hollar, Medallions by Van Lochem. This silhouette illustrates the typical line of a dress worn over the* vertugadin à tambour. *Leloir, "Histoire du Costume," Ernst, Paris.*

Figure 196. *This engraving by Franz Brun represents Frederick Henry, Prince of Orange, Frederick V of Bohemia, and Ernest Casimir of Nassau with their families. All of these costumes reveal the characteristics of the first period of the Seventeenth Century. Leloir, Galerie du Palais, Paris.*

Figure 197. *French costumes, 1630–1640, by St. Igny and Abraham Bosse. In the costumes of these four cavaliers we can observe variations and personal accents in breeches, collars, and cloaks. The gentleman second from the left displays the fashion of wearing several pair of hose at once; the top pair is finished with light* volants *which adorn the cupped cuff of the boot. His costume is trimmed with the ribbon decoration known as* petite oie. *Leloir, "Histoire du Costume," Ernst, Paris.*

At that time, the balloon-shaped breeches of the Sixteenth Century were used only by horsemen; the new breeches reached down to the knees in embroidered strips, braid, and ribbons. Men liked little, pointed beards and wore hats with tall crowns and narrow brims (Figure 196).

In a second style, men went without beards but had long, pointed moustaches. The jackets, longer now, were not cut at the waistline, but were marked there by knotted ribbons. The large collar was turned and called *rabat;* it was in lace, like the cuffs, or in silk when it was part of the shirt.

A little later, men let their hair grow longer, curled their moustaches, and wore a tiny beard, called the "fly" (Figure 197). Breeches also changed and throughout Europe took their name, *pantaloni,* and style from the famous actor of Venetian comedy, Pantalon, who was at that time playing successfully in Paris.

Figure 198. An old print depicting a school scene of the mid-Seventeenth Century. Again, we can observe that the children's costumes are similar to, but simpler than, those of the adults.

The Seventeenth Century

a

b

c

d

The Seventeenth Century 201

Figure 200. Portrait of Charles I *by the famous Flemish painter, Anthony Van Dyck (1599–1641). This portrait is a superb example of the elegant, but simpler, English taste. Louvre, Paris.*

The painters who described the costume during the reign of Louis XIII were many, especially the Flemish: Rubens, Rembrandt, Van Dyck, Hals; and the Frenchmen, Jacques Callot and Abraham Bosse (Figures 198, 199). Thanks to these great artists, this style was immortalized and remains the most typical of that century (Figure 200). In Spain, Velasquez became court painter to Phillip IV and described beautifully and authentically the costume of the Spanish nobility (Figure 201).

Meanwhile, women changed the line of their dresses with a new kind of vertugadin, *cache-enfant,* which determined an anti-esthetic silhouette by putting the waistline right under the bosom. With this style, the décolletage was open and hairdos enriched the sides of the head with curls.

In the Seventeenth Century, shoes developed really new lines and, for the first time, had heels. Men's shoes were especially affected and adorned with ribbons and soft cockades of satin (Figure 202). Gloves were widely used and particularly refined, and handkerchiefs, hanging from the pockets, were considered the most precious mark of male elegance.

Figure 202. *Some models of men's shoes from 1610 to 1640. It is interesting to note that many of the details are seen in women's shoes of today.*

Jewels were very elaborate. Ladies liked to wear large pearl necklaces and sophisticated watches; fans and heavy engraved crosses, elaborated by precious stone pendants, were popular.

Ladies and gentlemen then began to wear dressing gowns in splendid silks, embroidered with silver or gold braid; often the fabric was enriched by embroidered flower bouquets in delicate colors.

During the four years that separated styles determined by the vertugadin à tambour and the vertugadin cache-enfant, ladies preferred long skirts which had no evidence of reinforcements. Above these simply pleated skirts, they wore a light jacket encrusted with lace, called the *brassière* (Figure 203).

In this century, women in mourning wore black dresses; widows used a special rigid coiffe, completed with a black veil framed by a strip of brass or iron (Figure 204). A mourning style widely used in Holland and France between 1615 and 1640 was the *huiken*, which was a long, pleated veil-cloak that clung to the figure and reached to the floor. It was fixed on the forehead by the *houppe*, a unique headdress composed of a little wheel with a brush and flower in the center (Figure 205).

History of Fashions

Figure 204. *Engravings showing the front and back views of widow's weeds by St. Igny and Abraham Bosse. We see the* en conque *headdressing popular among the aristocracy. This costume is worn over the* vertugadin cache-enfant. *Leloir, "Histoire du Costume," Ernst, Paris.*

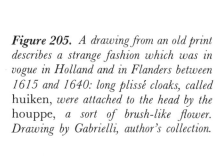

Figure 205. *A drawing from an old print describes a strange fashion which was in vogue in Holland and in Flanders between 1615 and 1640: long plissé cloaks, called* huiken, *were attached to the head by the* houppe, *a sort of brush-like flower. Drawing by Gabrielli, author's collection.*

Women's stockings were blue, green, red, black, or black with flowers; and the garters were of frilled gold lace with velvet ribbons. Men also used very sophisticated stockings. We can see in a painting by Francisco Zurbarán that they often wore several pair of hose at a time: a first pair in plain white linen, a second pair in embroidered batiste, a third of knitted silk, and finally a fourth of silk open-work or embroidered relief. Thus the legs seemed to blossom as from the petals of a rose (Figure 206). An original painter was the Spaniard Zurbarán; he was especially known for his religious paintings but he also made portraits of beautiful ladies of Seville in sumptuous dress, precious for fabric and jewels, but usually atypical of the time.

Muffs were used, generally of marten or sable, and parasols were carried for the ladies by pages. All the courts had pages; they were boys of good family, who, for four years, were educated physically and intellectually for this position. They were expected to be faithful to their patrons; they were not servants, but were only learning to become fine gentlemen. Their costumes always showed sophisticated and interesting styles, sometimes following current fashions, sometimes conceived with individual fantasy. At the Museum of Versailles, it is possible to see many costumes of pages, illustrated by Abraham Bosse and coming from the Castle of Richelieu. Famous is the *trousse* of pages, so-called because it was closed like a box. It was inspired by the balloon-shaped breeches of the Sixteenth Century (Figure 207).

A second long period for the evolution of costume in the Seventeenth Century started soon after Louis XIV, who was then only five years old, became King of France. Because he was a child, his influence on costume was not felt for some years. But soon the young gentlemen at court openly professed an interest in new fashions and laid down new laws of

Figure 207. *From a painting–engraving by St. Igny and Abraham Bosse we see typical costumes for pages. The characteristic breeches were named* trousse *for their box-like construction. Leloir, "Histoire du Costume," Ernst, Paris.*

Figure 206. *Portrait of the natural son of Philippe IV of Spain by Francisco Zurbarán (1598–1664). The young man wears a costume of white satin; interesting is the simple, straight line of the trousers. Several pair of stockings in fine linen flourish around his legs. Cavallo Collection, Chateau de Valandry, France.*

Figure 208. *This sketch taken from an old print describes with marvelous detail the sophisticated costume* en rhingrave *worn by Louis XIV of France. A flat hat, covered with* panaches, *rests on a wig* à fenêtres; *the rhingrave skirt covers full-knee breeches; and the entire ensemble is adorned with* petite oie dentelle, *expressing the ultimate in fashion caprice and exaggeration. Drawing by Gabrielli, author's collection.*

elegance. The most well known were Gaston Nogaret, Nompart de Caumont, the Marquis of Wardes, Villeroix, and Henry de Daillon. All invented and gave names to many new styles or accessories of costume. In that environment full of fanaticism the young king grew up, and during his youth the most fanciful fashions for men were conceived (Figure 208).

Hats flourished large brims covered with ostrich plumes, the *panaches,* which typified the exaggerated taste. Men's shirts were very refined and finished with precious *dentelles.* The jackets, when worn with the *rhingrave,* were short, like boleros. The rhingrave, a short skirt or skirtlike trousers worn over the breeches, took its name from the German *Rhein-Graf,* Earl of Rhine. It was, in fact, the brother of the Palatine Princess who introduced this creation to the court of France. The period of the rhingrave, 1650 to 1675, marked the triumph of a particular type of decorative trimming called *petite oie,* meaning "little duck," which consisted of many little curled ribbons of velvet or satin. In Paris, where the ribbon industry flourished, the petite oie adorned jackets and shirts, rhingrave and breeches, hats and stockings, gloves and shoes (Figure 209).

At the Court of Versailles, people became delirious over elegance and spent fortunes on their costumes, which often were embroidered with gold and precious stones. In fact, the finest expressions of the Baroque style were displayed at the Court of Versailles, where invention and caprice gave birth to the myth of Fashion. At the end of the century and at the beginning of the Eighteenth Century, too, a doll, the famous "Piavola de Franza," was used as the first vehicle of publicity for fashion; it traveled across the borders into many countries spreading the Parisian "word."

While the ladies were content with adding some postiches to their natural hair, men's vanity, reaching a peak of exaggeration, demanded the use of wigs; and they devised many

History of Fashions

Figure 209. *Procession of the Joiners of Frankfort, 1659. The joiners' corporations had a long tradition in Germany and commanded great respect, as we can see by these fine costumes with rhingrave and decorated with petit oie in the latest fashion. Leloir, "Histoire du Costume," Ernst, Paris.*

Figure 210. *A well-to-do couple in ceremonial attire by Van der Helst. He wears a black costume with rhingrave and a white shirt with large rabat; the lady has an unusual gown, simple and full of grace, and she carries a light ostrich feather as a fan. Her hairdo is en serpenteaux and she wears large, pendant pearl earrings. Leloir, "Histoires du Costume," Ernst, Paris.*

different types (Figure 210). The most monumental was called *en folio.* The conceited noblemen popularized the wearing of wigs when they discovered that the young sovereign had a magnificent head of hair. The *Roi Soleil* adopted wigs, but he did not like to renounce the exhibition of his own beautiful hair; so he invented and usually wore the so-called *perruque à fenêtres,* which was made out of a light *canepin* with holes for inserting the real hair.

The Seventeenth Century   **209**

In this grandiose century, the cloak also took on an unusual importance and was used not just for warmth, but very often to express the manners of the time. For example, when they visited a house in mourning, men would leave their cloaks as homage to the dead. At church they assisted in the celebration of Mass with cloak and hat on; if they were in a restaurant with ladies, they left the cloak draped over the back of the chair and raised their hats when they drank to them. In other words, in the Seventeenth Century cloaks were used ceremoniously; they were made and draped in many different styles, each with a different name and distinct use (Figure 211).

Boots were in common use. High and low, with tops folded over or falling cuplike, they were made in plain, natural-colored leather or in red, black, and white, embroidered in silver and gold (Figure 212). Shoes, too, were often made in white, red, or brown leather, or in broadcloth and velvets.

Figure 211. *Two versions of the* hongreline. *(Upper) A detail from the "Siège de Privas" by Prévost shows the Cardinal de Richelieu on horseback in the type of coat which he would wear in the field. (Lower) An engraving by Callot presents a gentleman in a typical* hongreline, *a type of coat that took its name from Hungary and replaced the doublet. Musée de Versailles.*

Figure 212. Several models of boots from 1620 to 1630. All of them are spurred; some of them have the tops reversed upon themselves showing decorative stockings with scalloped, lace trimming. Leloir, "Histoire du Costume," Ernst, Paris.

If the feminine hairdressings were simpler than the men's, they were nevertheless sophisticated in this century; and, as with many other modes and accessories of costume, their names were adapted from those of the ladies and gentlemen who popularized the styles. The *coiffeur en bouffons* (having two bunches of curls at the sides of the head) was very popular and was called *à la Sévigné* from Mme. de Sévigné as she appears in the portrait of Nanteuil in 1665 (Figure 213d). In many portraits, Trouvain recorded the popularity of the hairstyle *en Fontanges,* named after one of the King's mistresses but made famous by Mme. de Maintenon. In one painting she wears a little scarf of lightweight black silk on this hairdo; that style, which became very common at the end of this century, was called *ténèbres* and often was worn with a little black mask on the face.

Figure 213. Fashionable hairdos: (a) Marie Thérèse and (b) Dorothée de Buwinchausen, coiffured à la hurluberlu; *(c) the Duchess of Longueville; (d) the Marquise of Sévigné* en bouffon, *from a portrait by Nanteuil (1665); (e) Madame de Montespan coiffured* en serpenteaux.

The Seventeenth Century   **211**

Figure 215. *Among feminine fashion accessories, the* pièces d'estomac *were very useful for women who could alter the appearance of a dress by varying these additions. This* pièce *is of white satin embroidered in gold; the small flaps were used to attach it to the corset.*

Figure 214. Engraving from the journal "Mercure Galant" of 1678, illustrating a men's fashion boutique in which we can observe skirts rhingrave, gloves, cravats, hose, shoes, wigs, and other fashionable accessories. Leloir, "Histoire du Costume," Ernst, Paris.

There came into fashion some special gloves which were cut so as to leave the fingertips bare; these were the *mitaines,* made of velvet or silk, embroidered and decorated. The mitaines would return in the Eighteenth Century made in silk or fur, and again in the Nineteenth Century made of a *filet* net of silk. Gloves in general were very refined and, from some fine ladies, were called *à la Neroli, à la Frangipane,* and so on.

We know all the extravagant modes of Versailles from the *Mercure Galant* which was founded in Paris by de Visé in 1672. This journal was the first to report on fashion and it paid particular attention to the capricious "high life" at the Court of Versailles (Figure 214). In 1714 it was renamed *Mercure de France* and was the oldest of French newspapers after the *Gazette de France.*

This century introduced the first fine fashion shops where it was possible to buy all the elegant accessories, such as cravats, rabats, muffs, cuffs, coiffes, gloves, bandoliers, and, for the ladies, the so-called *pièces d'estomac*—changeable parts of bodices which they used to transform their dresses and give them different importance and aspects (Figure 215). The finest boutique was the "Galerie du Palais Royal," patronized by the most elegant ladies and gentlemen of Paris.

The center of elegance was Paris, and the affected style was that of the Court of Versailles. French painting, however, appeared to be still a slave of Flemish influence. Indeed, in Paris Flemish *tapissiers* dominated the field of tapestry making, and Flemish painters flourished not only in Paris, but also in Lyon, Toulouse, and Bordeaux. The most beautiful French portraits were from the hands of Flemish masters, such as Frans Pourbus, Phillippe de Champaigne, Anthony Van Dyck, and the Dutch Vermeer (Figure 216).

Figure 216. In Young Woman with a Water Jug, *Jan Vermeer (1632–1675) embodies the dignity and simplicity of the Dutch middle class. The Metropolitan Museum of Art, Gift of Henry G. Marguand, 1889.*

Figure 217. *An engraving by Stefano della Bella in 1646 pictures bourgeoises strolling on the Pont Neuf in Paris. The women wear white linen pèlerine collars, known as the* berta, *and their heads are covered with black kerchiefs knotted under the chin.*

But, in the theater, France produced Corneille and presented Molière, who polemized with the "Sun King" and his fanciful court. From the stage, in fact, Molière started to unveil the parody of that society with his witty masks and began to stylize the characters he liked to criticize. In this way he also started the movement to free the theater from superficial fashions and to construct authentic personalities, setting the figures against their historical background.

Later came an edict banning the use of precious metals and stones in dress embroidery. But the ineffable King tried in vain to cultivate a simpler taste, for he offered as a prize to the most deserving courtiers the right to wear special waistcoats: the famous *justaucorp à brevet,* most preciously embroidered and autographed with the signature of the King. The design of this lavish waistcoat changed according to the current fashion, but it was always exclusively in "royal blue,"

History of Fashions

lined in red, with embroideries in silver and gold. To be given this privilege became the great ambition of the courtiers; however, only fifty were granted by the sovereign.

Men's fashions in the second half of this century, then, originated at Versailles and were castigated by Molière. His sharp and subtle wit gradually but surely persuaded the fashion fanatics to abandon their exaggerations.

Ladies no longer used reinforcements for their skirts (Figure 217). Instead, they wore three skirts of which the first was in heavy white cotton, flat in front and deeply pleated around the hips and back, determining the new silhouette. Over that *dessous,* fine ladies wore dresses in light fabrics, decorated with a special kind of volants, called falbalas. Those dresses were usually worn with original hairdos. One of them, mentioned earlier, involving a crest of ribbons or lace fixed by jewels on a small bonnet, was created by Marie Angelique Scoraille de Fontanges and bore her name (Figures 218, 219).

Figure 218. An engraving by Bonnart of a shoemaker's shop. The lady trying on shoes is coiffed en fontanges, *while the shoemaker wears the wig* en folio. *Cabinet des Estampes, Paris.*

Figure 219. An elegant lady wears a costume richly adorned with ermine. The ténèbre, *a filmy black veil introduced by Madame de Maintenon, complements the white headdress en fontanges. Drawing by Gabrielli, author's collection.*

Figure 220. *This drawing describes the typical dress* en falbalas *which came into fashion in the last years of the Seventeenth Century. Drawing by Gabrielli, author's collection.*

Figure 221. *Sketch of the costume* à la Teckeli, *in fashion around 1695, shows the Marechal de Luxembourg in civilian dress with touches of the military. The exaggerated fur muff became a popular fashion accessory for men. Drawing by Gabrielli, author's collection.*

Fashionable later were rich skirts with falbalas turning up in the back and imitating in front an apron; behind, a bizarre, rooster-shaped motif was created. That style was the mode after 1680, when the pièce d'estomac had become very common (Figure 220).

At the end of this century, as we will see again at the end of the Eighteenth and Nineteenth Centuries, the feminine fashion appeared much simplified. It seemed to be a reaction to past excesses, seeking simpler forms to create the silhouette. And although each is one hundred years apart from the other, these lines are strangely similar.

A sense of boredom also developed in men's styles, and a craving for something new became manifest. Men who had worn huge wigs now adopted the simplest type, called *à la brigadière*. They used, above all, the redingotes, but also they wore long, embroidered waistcoats, sometimes closed by buttons; and they liked a leather belt with an elegant muff hanging from it. For a hat, they preferred the tricorne (Figure 221). Soft shirts with cravats *à la Steinkerque* completed their attire. On the whole, they preserved their sophistication in many ways, but they exchanged their complicated lines for simpler ones and thereby announced the beginning of the Eighteenth Century (Figure 222).

With the Seventeenth Century a long historical cycle of centuries came to an end. It was a cycle that began with the splendors of the Byzantine Empire and continued through the magnificence of the Renaissance era, when the concept of wealth was equivalent to an accumulation of gold and precious stones. Consequently, costume also had been exceptionally sumptuous, with its display of jewels reaching a level of luxury difficult to imagine today.

In the Sixteenth Century, the term "Barocco" had been used to indicate a sort of deceit; while in the Eighteenth Cen-

Figure 222. After 1692, in commemoration of a battle victory, the cravate à la Steinkerque *became fashionable. Men knotted loosely a long length of silk or lace around their necks and pulled the ends through a buttonhole of the redingote. Drawing by Gabrielli, author's collection.*

tury, writers used it in a derogatory sense. But applied to the men of the Seventeenth Century, it can only be used with a sense of admiration. The great Baroque artists mastered all the techniques inherited from the Renaissance but used them with a different spirit. They seemed to need to engender wonder in the viewer in order to nudge him past the limitations of form and color. Perhaps, as the prominent Italian art historian, Lionello Venturi, has so aptly written, their breaking open of cupolas and vaults to reveal "Paradise" was a typical result of the "esthetics of deceit." Viewing their art, one has the impression of a fantasy amazingly alive, yet not satisfied with reality—even when it resorts to tricks or *trompe-l'œil* effects.

From that dissatisfaction came the uncertainty which set the Seventeenth Century apart from two epochs of clearly defined cultural style: the Renaissance and Illuminism, a cultural movement of the Eighteenth Century which encouraged reason to liberate men from superstition. The baroque imagination has been compared to fretfulness of thought; and many things foreseen in the Renaissance became anguish in the Seventeenth Century. But if that anguish often induced errors of taste, it also gave this century a singular value. The *Seicento* left a great heritage to the succeeding evolution of art.

The Eighteenth Century

It was the Eighteenth Century which laid the ground for modern progress; in every field of knowledge there was a need and a search for a necessary evolution. Political ideals seemed finished in the upheaval of governments, the constantly changing successions, the slavery of Austria and Spain. Also the Renaissance ideal of an heroic humanity was crushed; but fortunately it was preserved among a small elite, destined to be regenerated later.

The mode of expression changed again: at the beginning of the century the Barocco style became lighter and glided into a new kind of decoration characterized by a general affirmation of the French taste. It would retain the scenographic grandeur from Barocco, but beyond that it would develop a gentle expression of elegance, marking a first reaction to the rules and formalities of the Seventeenth Century. In a certain sense, the shifting emphasis was an announcement of the overwhelming changes we find at the end of this century.

219

French

French

The new style that would be called *Rococo* was sometimes a kind of refined Baroque, lightly flourished and often too affected. Fashionable in France during the reign of Louis XV, Rococo actually dominated just the end of the first half of the Eighteenth Century. After that came many changes in the history of art and civilization as new horizons opened up with the excavations which brought to light the cities of Pompeii and Herculaneum and gave birth to the science of archaeology.

In the Eighteenth Century, out of the still life of Seicento paintings, came the landscape. No longer a distant background, it moved forward and became important in itself. Giorgione's *Tempest,* in which he presents the landscape as a protagonist, is a famous example of this new emphasis.

The artist most characteristic of his age is the great French painter Antoine Watteau. He created a poetic world where the *fêtes galantes* were celebrated with splendor. But the world of Watteau exceeds the limits of the style of his epoch because he found a mystic paradise where youth, beauty, and sensuality seem to ignore the existence of passing time. Thus, elegantly displaying only the best of their beauty, he concealed the passing of two centuries and styles of art. A delicate painter of costume, Watteau deliberately ignored artificial inventions or exaggerations of fashion, such as the vertugadin or *panier,* when painting the feminine silhouette (Figure 223).

A finesse and a touch of fantasy were added to the dramatic movement of Seventeenth-Century painting. The violent contrasts of *chiaroscuro* created in the paintings of Caravaggio and Ribera seemed dissolved in a serene atmosphere in which all was light.

The figures of Tiepolo, famous Venetian painter, are literally drenched with light, and everything in his frescoes seems to reflect the luminous skies which he used as backgrounds. His frescoes seem to be windows opened in the sky. Giambattista Tiepolo was an unsurpassed "colorist" who renewed in Venice the glory of Paolo Veronese. He created also a series of paintings called *pulcinellate* which were amusing, decorative escapes and an interpretation of the naiveté of the masks of Commedia dell'Arte. As on the stage, it was customary to repeat in one painting the same mask and the same costume, only showing different attitudes and expressions (Figure 224).

Besides Tiepolo, there were many other Venetian painters who described that city in the Eighteenth Century. Illustrating in *genre* paintings the picturesque life of the merriest city in Italy were Canaletto, Guardi, and Longhi, and all were masters of costume. In some of Longhi's paintings we can see a particular Venetian costume made of two skirts, one hanging down and the other brought up over the head like a shawl. The white cotton dress, often worn with red velvet slippers, was a popular costume of the time.

Figure 224. Detail from Il Pagliaccio Innamorato *by Giovanni Domenico Tiepolo (1727–1804) in which we see typical masks and costumes of the Commedia dell'Arte. Ca' Rezzonico, Venice.*

The Eighteenth Century

221

Figure 225. In this painting by Pietro Longhi (1702–1785), we can clearly observe the details of the tabarro, the bauta in black lace, and the characteristic masks in rigid, white cotton or silk. Ca' Rezzonico, Venice.

Longhi sometimes shows a special cloak that was an imitation of a fashion from the end of the Seventeenth Century—a cloak with a cape, called *tabarro* (Figure 225). It was usually black or scarlet, in fine cloth or wool, with a little collar in velvet or satin; sometimes it was lined in fur, sometimes in colored silk. During the summer the tabarro was white or yellow gold. One of the characteristics of Venetian fashion is the *bauta*. In a certain sense replacing the touret of the Renaissance, it consisted of a sort of cowl adherent to the head, in black silk or lace, falling to the elbow, and worn with the tricorn. It was fashionable to wear a mask, not just for parties and balls, but also to go out in town or to travel incognito. Very common was a caricaturing mask in rigid white cotton or silk, and another, in black velvet or satin, covering nose and eyes.

In the theater, the *Commedia di Costume* assumed an ethical content and sought to express the travail of Eighteenth-Century society, which later and inevitably found its outlet in the French Revolution. Goldoni transferred this reality to the stage. The theatrical organization developed more precise outlines, conceived in a critical and cultural search. Great painters, such as the French Boucher and Nadal Canziani of Venice, gave new refinements to the theatrical costume and interpreted the text with fresh historical sensitivity, gently adjusting costume to the character.

Despite the modernization of the theater, there was an unpleasant contrast between costumes worn by secondary actors and the sumptuous ones worn by leading actors whose elegant costumes were presented to them by members of high society with whom they had *liaisons amoureuses*. In contrast with established companies protected by the courts, streets and theaters were populated by wandering actors, strolling minstrels who did not think about the problem of equipment.

They could have been the same pathetic comics used by Shakespeare as creatures in a "Midsummer Night's Dream," or those so well described by Cervantes or Sorel.

François Boucher was another exponent of the frivolous, gay, and licentious life of Louis XV's court. His art is representative of that *Rocaille* style which takes its name (as does Rococo itself) from the rocks and shells Boucher used in his mythological paintings. Later, he used them in many paintings to symbolize the lightness of forms in general. Rocaille likewise became a characteristic of some feminine fashions of this century and it was a typical embellishment of the applied arts such as tapestry and porcelain. Boucher's portrait of Antoinette Poisson, Madame de Pompadour, is a fine expression of the Rocaille style in painting and costume (Figure 226). The favorite of Louis XV, Madame de Pompadour was a woman of great political influence and a generous patroness of the arts.

New ideas of line and color appeared in fashion also: one popular style was that of aprons, very finely embroidered, used as decoration for some fine dresses (Figure 227). While the elegant aprons of ladies were decorated by *ruches* and little flowers, the servants' aprons were very simple and practical. The aprons frequently inspired the French painter Fragonard, who graciously reinterpreted the style as he prolonged the carefree frivolity of earlier years into the second half of the century. Jean Honoré Fragonard also was considered something of a phenomenon in the world of art for he was able to paint his exquisite portraits with "sittings" of just one hour!

Figure 226. Portrait of Antoinette Poisson, Madame de Pompadour, *by François Boucher (1703–1770). Politically influential, this elegant beauty was also a generous patron of the arts. Her costume is an expressive illustration of the* rocaille *style of which Boucher is an acknowledged master. National Gallery, Edinburgh.*

Figure 227. *Drawn from an engraving of English ladies in promenade costume. In the center we see the decorative apron, a motif which recurs frequently in ladies' fashions of this century. The hairstyling and bonnets are still of modest proportions. Drawing by Gabrielli, author's collection.*

Figure 228. Two engravings illustrating the new lines of the early Eighteenth Century. On the left, from Antoine Watteau, is a typical example of the robe battante; *sometimes called an "Adrienne" after the actress Adrienne Lecouvreur, it was the first kind of* robe manteau. *On the right, from Bernard Picard, is a model of the* robe ajustée. Leloir, *"Histoire du Costume," Ernst, Paris.*

Ladies wore a special at-home dress, soft and free, called *déshabillé-négligé,* which consisted generally of a long embroidered shirt over which they wore a loose corset, called *gourgandine.* A coiffe in lace and a large dressing gown in brocade completed this comfortable costume.

In the beginning of this century it was common to wear ample capes bordered with fringe and embroideries, still baroque in taste. But, at the same time, the beautiful *robe battante* was created, which was a sort of *robe-manteau,* the simple, elegant, sumptuous garb that Antoine Watteau immortalized. Many styles were taken from his paintings and were called after him *à la Watteau* (Figure 228).

In speaking about the line of feminine dresses after 1725, we must consider the dessous and, then, the paniers which caused so many changes in the silhouette. Corsets, expertly and elaborately boned, determined the smooth fit of the bodices. Often they were covered with rich materials, such as brocade or damask, and were meant to be seen beneath the lacing or other closures; sometimes, a pièce d'estomac

History of Fashions

was pinned to a simpler corset to form the front of the bodice. Full petticoats of matching fabrics, or sometimes of quilted satin, enriched and filled out the skirt.

The first type of panier was conical, a rigid bell over which fell the skirt of the *trapèze* dress (Figure 229). The feminine silhouette appeared gracious and younger in that loose, charming dress, trapezoidal in shape, with entire sleeves fitted to the arms and ending in rich volants of lace at the elbows. The deep, ample décolletages were enriched by massive necklaces of corals and drop-shaped pearls, which produced an original effect in relief. More than two centuries later, in 1958, Yves Saint Laurent, the successor of Dior, found inspiration from that style.

Figure 229. This design from a 1736 engraving representing Mademoiselle Margot "fabricante de paniers et vendeuse," shows the first style of paniers *and the graceful line of dresses adapted to it. It is the same* trapèze *silhouette that inspired Yves St. Laurent in 1957. Drawing by Gabrielli, author's collection.*

Figure 230. From the French painter Cochin, some court costumes of 1745. Here we see the silhouette created by the second type of panier with extreme lateral extensions. The skirts conceived to cover up the angularities of the panier are made with overlapping volants, resembling the petals of a flower. The hairdo, too, has become more elaborate, enriched with long curls hanging down the back. Author's collection.

But soon the paniers became ridiculous. They extended the skirts enormously at the hips and consequently determined a new carriage on the part of the ladies. After 1750, the skirts appeared to be made out of lace petals; they were very slender at the waistline, and a long train, starting from the pointed bodice, cascaded to the floor. In his portraits, the French painter Cochin illustrated this period which was very interesting for its fabrics (Figure 230).

At that time, special light fabrics were preferred, gold and silver flowers embroidered on delicate backgrounds, taffetas worked in squares and called *étoffes à miroirs,* and white *moires* striped in pastel colors. For the winter, ladies dressed in cut velvets with designs in relief; for summer, in light taffetas striped in silver with little embroidered bouquets of silver flowers, or white *mousselines* sprinkled with tiny bunches of embroidered flowers. The stockings were crocheted, both white and colored; and shoes, with high heels, were made of silk, velvet, or embroidered light leather (Figure 231).

History of Fashions

Figure 231. *From Baudouin, Moreau le Jeune, and Boucher, three examples of the* robe relevée dans les poches *of 1755. The fullness of the overdress is charmingly gathered into special pockets cut in the sides of the dress. Engraving from author's collection.*

Figure 232. Atelier of Arles *showing young couturières at work. Their simple dresses, completed with a* fichu *at the neckline, show an interesting variety of fabrics and decorative designs; charming bonnets cover their heads. From the Library of the Accademia Italiana di Costume, Rome.*

Very much in demand were the cottons from India, called *furies,* with flowers and multicolored designs. The Indian cottons were contraband and, until 1860, had to be smuggled across borders; but in France, with the help of clever textile artists, the first *rouleau-cliché* was invented in 1775 and launched the industry of printed fabrics (Figure 232).

Madame de Pompadour spread the taste of Chinese motifs, and immediately the whole, ineffable feminine world was full of strange flowers and birds; Chinese magicians, dragons, pagodas appeared on dresses, tapestries, furniture, curtains, and fans.

Later, feminine hairdos were enriched with curls, postiches, cockades, feathers, birds, and grapes, until they became full of frivolities made from white powder and fantasies. Consequently, the coiffes and hats, which in the beginning of the century were modest in shape and decoration, also assumed monumental proportions and the most unbelievable shapes of castles, baskets of flowers, or caravelles with many sails (Figures 233, 234). Depain, who was a famous specialist in hairstyles in the final years before the outbreak of the French

Figure 234. *A sketch from a portrait by Orme illustrating an English interpretation of French styles. Drawing by Gabrielli, author's collection.*

Figure 233. *French costumes of 1773–1775 from water-color paintings of Carmontelle. The popularity of* taffetas *is demonstrated by these three striped dresses. The ladies having tea in the garden display an amusing group of hairdos. Engraving from author's collection.*

Figure 235. Mrs. Grace Dalrymple Elliott *by Thomas Gainsborough (1727– 1788). This portrait presents a sophisticated hairdo and an elegant dress that expresses the refined, simpler taste of the English fashions. Metropolitan Museum of Art, New York, bequest of William K. Vanderbilt, 1920.*

Figure 236. *Three costumes illustrating some of the fashions popular in the 1780's. On the left is the typical* robe en chemise, *in dotted* mousseline; *the huge headdress is probably of taffetas, trimmed with plumes and the same dotted fabric. The lady carries a large muff of Mongolian goat. In the center, a dress* à la lévite *is worn over the* faux cul; *a decorative apron, a shawl trimmed with* ruches, *and a broadrimmed hat complete this costume. The bustle silhouette is seen again on the right in the* robe à la turque. *This dress is made of* pékin *and garnished with ribbons and flowers. The large bonnet is encircled with little roses and crowned with plumes. Engraving from author's collection.*

Revolution, found it amusing to give strange titles to his creations, such as: *Coiffure sans Redoute,* which was, on the contrary, very well fortified with a wall of ribbons and laces; *Coiffure à l'Espoir,* with leaves in a sprinkling of green, the color of hope; *Chambre de la Liberté,* full of affected motifs; and the *Coiffure à la Nation,* displaying the colors of France (Plate 8).

In 1774, the feminine costume had assumed the greatest splendor of dentelles, embroideries, immeasurable paniers, and huge, tall, sophisticated wigs (Figure 235). The muffs became larger and were made out of monkey fur, chicken feathers, and embroidered silk. The hats were tricornered or large with tremendous, softly curled crowns in silk or velvet (Figure 236).

At about 1780, the court of Marie Antoinette was influenced by Spanish fashions and ladies wore *caracos,* a sort of jacket, fitted in front and usually loose behind, ending with ruches.

The Eighteenth Century   **233**

Later, English fashion, seeking to simplify the French line, introduced the so-called *robe à l'anglaise*, consisting of a little jacket and a soft skirt worn over a petticoat which, in the rear below the waistline, had a small cushion of horsehair, known as *cul de Paris*. The robe à l'anglaise sometimes was a two-piece creation with contrasting colors, but almost always it was completed by white *fichus*. Fragonard liked to portray these interesting styles too (Figure 237). For the young ladies it was also smart to wear the *robes en chemise*, a completely loose, shirtlike creation in light fabrics, fixed at the waist by satin or taffetas ribbons.

In the Eighteenth Century women used a heavy makeup, called *fard*, which became fashionable especially after the epidemic of smallpox from which Louis XV died.

For about ten years before the Revolution, there was the amusing habit of giving different names to the innumerable styles of feminine dresses. Names like à la francaise, à l'anglaise, à la polonaise, à la czarine, à la circassienne, à la turque, à la levite really involved almost the same line, changing only the kind of decoration.

Figure 237. The Stolen Kiss *by Jean Honoré Fragonard (1732–1806). This famous painting presents a costume of elegant simplicity: the dress of pale blue satin has fitted sleeves and the typical pointed bodice. A light fichu of gaze is carelessly knotted in front and an overdress of darker satin provides contrast; a striped stole of transparent material completes the costume of the young lady. Her simple hairdo would seem to date this scene prior to the extravagances of Marie Antoinette's court, but the* fichu *is a detail characteristic of the reign of Louis XVI. The Hermitage, Leningrad.*

French

Figure 238. *Several hairdressings popular in Marie Antoinette's epoch. (a) From a painting by Moreau le Jeune, waved natural hair and layered curls are surmounted by a crest of ostrich plumes. (b) Marie Antoinette with powdered hair and a postiche of curls topped by a huge knot of striped taffetas and feathers. (c) Coiffure* en hérisson. *This original style was created by stiffening the hair so that it stood up in spikes; then ribbons, feathers, and fantasies were added. (d) Towering hairdo with pouf of taffetas and flowers. (e) The Princess of Lamballe with large wig crowned by a garland of flowers. (f) Coiffure* en colisée, *a well-supported, sophisticated confection. Engraving from author's collection.*

Cochin and Moreau the Young demonstrated a particular facility for reproducing in their portraits the original, refined hairdos of this period which, by the way, had sophisticated titles, such as *Hèrisson* and *Colisée* (Figure 238).

Figure 239. Costumes of footmen redrawn from a fashion magazine of 1726 in which the redingote motif is repeated. The tricorne was the popular hat for men from the early part of the century until the 1780's. Drawings by Gabrielli, author's collection.

Ladies' muffs now became enormous and were made of swan, Siberian wolf, or Angora goat. Many exquisite jewels were used as accessories, as were canes, umbrellas, snuff boxes, watches, chains, fine gloves, miniatures, lorgnettes, and pendants hanging from the neck on velvet ribbons.

The preferred colors for male attire were green, tobacco, and gold. The favorite fabric was *drap* (broadcloth); and that from Sedan was particularly famous. Men wore picturesque cloaks and embroidered waistcoats. The typical hat was the tricorne, and the cravat was sometimes part of the shirt, tied and falling in a vaporous jabot.

Trousers were tightly fitted and reached to the knee (Figure 239). And stockings, earlier in white silk, later became colored, black, and even striped. The waistcoats were given a coquettish air with their designs of landscapes, stylized animals, and delicate floral patterns. Made out of damask or velvet, they were completed with buttons of gold, silver, or enamel. And shoe heels became lower.

Men's wigs, created under Louis XIV, the "Sun King," were used in the Eighteenth Century also. In about 1680, wigs had been monumental, but later, they gradually became more modest until, finally, in 1750, they were gathered at the base of the neck in a little bag of black silk tied with a knot, which made a nice contrast with the white jabot (Figure 240). At home, men also used berets in velvet or silk, ornamented with fur or *pompons*.

In 1750 and afterward, perhaps influenced by ladies' paniers, the men's redingotes were enriched at the sides by groups of pleats (Figure 241). Later men's fashions assumed unusually feminine characteristics, with a long redingote, sometimes

Figure 240. From the Encyclopedie *of Diderot. The atelier of a wigmaker showing popular Eighteenth Century styles for men.*

Figure 241. Men's redingotes, influenced by the line of the ladies' paniers, are enriched at the hips by groups of pleats. Engraving from author's collection.

Figure 242. *Elegant gentleman in promenade dress; his long redingote, high boots, crowned hat, and huge fur muff are the ultimate in fashion for 1789. Author's collection.*

Figure 243. *Men's fashions from 1789 to 1791 from the "Magasin des Modes." Here we can see the new styles in hats, wigs, and the many effeminate details of the fashions. The gilet, and tight buttoned knee breeches are now worn under the elongated redingotes. Author's collection.*

opened in front and showing embroidered waistcoats, striped stockings, and huge muffs of fur or brown wool tied with colorful knots (Figures 242, 243).

England had created the redingote. Originally a riding coat or sports jacket, it later was considered especially fitting as a ceremonial coat. Priests wore a short redingote with buttons in front; and a round cloak of Seventeenth-Century taste topped it, flowing down and back from the shoulders.

Gloves were usually white, sometimes gold fringed. Canes generally were made of *rodin,* a special Indian wood, with the head in gold, silver, agate, or ivory with little precious stones.

The Revolution arrived violently and terrifyingly, as a gigantic force to demolish all the past and, seemingly, destroy all traditional civilization, all privileges, beliefs, and social disparities. From the ideal of the Revolution came the idea of the Empire, which was a Roman idea; the Republican convention produced Napoleon and the European struggle for the supremacy of France.

The dress of the revolutionary man was completely new and different: he wore a short jacket called *carmagnole,* and the first type of long trousers, a red scarf, and beret.

Women of the Revolution adopted large skirts without reinforcements; as a hat, the soft *charlotte* in lace, or a simple cloche with a red cockade, leaving the natural hair loosened on the shoulders. And the light fichu embraced the bodice and tied in the back.

Figure 244. *Promenade costumes of the Directoire period. The gentlemen are dressed* à l'Incroyable *and the lady, as seen from her exaggerated styles, is a* Merveilleuse. *Drawings by Gabrielli, author's collection.*

Meanwhile, in the common male costume, such frivolities as ribbons, embroideries, nonfunctional buttons, galoons, and fantasy in fabrics disappeared. The long jackets were now somewhere between the redingote and the frock; with the fitted trousers, now calf length, they used boots with folded tops in different colors.

In contrast, the *Incroyables* (as the name implies) prolonged their unbelievable styles, adopting the highest collars of all the epochs, and light-weight, long cravats wrapped around the neck. They wore hairdos *en oreilles de chien* and exaggerated hats, all in keeping with the *Merveilleuses'* eccentric styles (Figures 244, 245).

History of Fashions

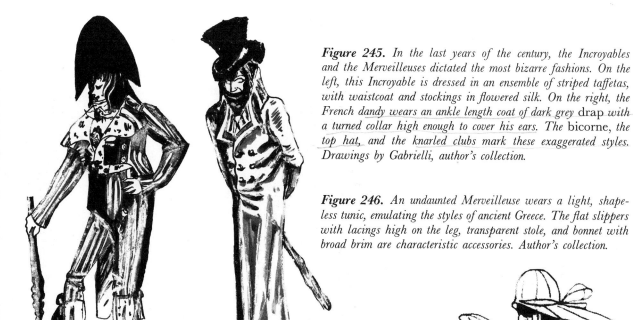

Figure 245. In the last years of the century, the Incroyables and the Merveilleuses dictated the most bizarre fashions. On the left, this Incroyable is dressed in an ensemble of striped taffetas, with waistcoat and stockings in flowered silk. On the right, the French dandy wears an ankle length coat of dark grey drap with a turned collar high enough to cover his ears. The bicorne, the top hat, and the knarled clubs mark these exaggerated styles. Drawings by Gabrielli, author's collection.

Figure 246. An undaunted Merveilleuse wears a light, shapeless tunic, emulating the styles of ancient Greece. The flat slippers with lacings high on the leg, transparent stole, and bonnet with broad brim are characteristic accessories. Author's collection.

The Merveilleuses, who were intellectual and liberated women, adopted exaggerated styles derived from classic models of antiquity, both in dress and in modes of living. They wore veils and used particular coiffes with long braids; carrying little bags called *reticules,* they wore flat, laced slippers and particularly liked transparent tunics showing, at the sides, the naked legs. Light stoles and charming parasols completed this "casual" attire (Figure 246).

The macabre idea of the guillotine suggested to women the fashion *à la victime,* which consisted of a red ribbon tied around the neck. High-society fashions repeated the characteristics of those formerly worn by the common people. Even the fabrics

The Eighteenth Century   **241**

Figure 247. Portrait of Madame de Seriziat *by Jacques Louis David (1748–1845). In a light robe en chemise, softly gathered and belted at the natural waistline with a ribbon, Mme. de Seriziat presents a picture of contrived, Neoclassic simplicity. The brim of her beribboned hat is lined with a crisp white volant. Louvre, Paris.*

Figure 248. Portrait of Monsieur de Seriziat *by David. This gentleman's costume embodies the finest elements of the 1795 style without the foppishness so often present. Louvre, Paris.*

were much alike: no more silks and damasks, but cloth of cotton, linen, gauze, white or printed for women; wool or leather for men (Figures 247, 248).

Napoleon moved in the name of principles and directed his bold enterprises as a war of peoples, claiming rights for their oppressed nationality. He was thus able to arrive as a liberator to restore the Roman Empire and, with it, a bulwark of liberty and justice. From this concept would germinate all modern history, which, meanwhile, was diffused in the vast breadth of classicism renewed in the arts. Napoleon was enraptured with "Romanity." In his dreams of the Empire, he wanted to have all the decorations recreated in the style of Greek and Roman orders of old, and he encouraged artists to work in the style now known as Neo-Classicism.

Tailors and costumers also were inspired by the classic models. And actors assumed the motifs for new fashions, called archaeological, because they were directly inspired by that new science. Naturally, all the theatrical repertory was again dedicated primarily to Greek and Roman subjects.

The Eighteenth Century 243

Figure 249. Portrait of the Marquesa de Pontejos *by Goya. In this painting the treatment of the fabrics is extraordinary! Using all the nuances of the color of a tearose, from golden yellow to pale pink, Goya makes us feel the light crispness of the organdy and taffetas. National Gallery of Art, Washington, D. C.*

Figure 250. Portrait of Don Manuel de la Peña *by Francisco de Goya (1746–1828). This velvet court costume is garnished with gold braid and gold buttons close the waistcoat. The outer coat, probably derived from the redingote, has developed something of the cutaway line. Courtesy of the Hispanic Society of America, New York.*

The greatest tragic author and actor of the time, Joseph Talma, renewed the dramatic arts and realized a deeper reform of the theatrical costume. Thus Neo-Classicism restored to costume its function of historical characterization.

In 1793, from Talma's tragedy *Bérénice,* the ladies adopted the *coiffure à la Titus* with hair cut extremely short all around. This style rapidly passed from fashion, and they resorted to postiches and even little wigs for the festive occasions of the First Empire.

The Neo-Classic movement, in the name of ancient culture, was able to reestablish in the general taste and in art the balance and rhythm which seemed to have been swept away by the invasion of the Baroque style.

Only in Spain was the new movement resisted. Francisco Goya, Spain's greatest painter since Velasquez, was not impressed by Neo-Classicism. In 1780 he was appointed as court painter to Charles IV and there achieved his first success as a portraitist. He left many important paintings illustrating the Spanish costume of the time (Figures 249, 250). In 1792 he became deaf after an illness, and this was the period in which

The Eighteenth Century

he engraved the famous *Caprichos,* a series of etchings which seem to have come from an unreal, fantastic world of monsters and specters. The death of the Duchess of Alba brought him great unhappiness; and then the suffering of his people during the war affected him deeply. To express the national mourning, he engraved the *Disasters of War,* which commemorated the bloody days of the resistance of Madrid against Napoleon. From that moment, his art became dramatic and expressionistic and seemed to represent a movement both bold and original.

The French Revolution had suddenly put an end to all the masks, carnivals, fêtes galantes, the comedies of Goldoni, the librettos of Metastasio, and the music of Mozart. All that fantasy of colors and ornaments which had extensively represented the Rococo and the *Settecento* seemed to be torn away, but not completely terminated. Perhaps it could be the only acceptable end for a century like the Settecento, for the charm and levity of Rococo was a superficial mask, so diluting to the traditions of the Eighteenth Century that its aspirations and genius are incomprehensible to us. The Settecento, however, remains as a smile of the past; the smile of an overwrought humanity.

The Nineteenth Century

A French painter, Jacques Louis David, can be considered the apostle of the new style that had invaded the artistic manifestations of every field. David was forty-one years old when the Revolution broke out in France, and for a long time he was by far the most elegant interpreter of the costume that had been disrupted by the Revolution, sophisticated by the Directoire, and emphasized by Napoleon (Figure 251). He also painted enormous canvases singing the glories of the Empire and the refined elegance of the court.

At that time there appeared several fashion magazines in Paris, Florence, and Venice; and they faithfully reported the fashion that David idealized in his portraits (Figures 252a–j).

Personally, Napoleon liked to dress very simply, wearing the colonel's uniforms in dark green drap with red collar and cuffs. He turned up the brim of his hat and thereby set a style which is still called the "Napoleonic hat." His frock coat was blue with a white collar and the "Eagle of the Legion" was embroidered in silver and gold on the breast.

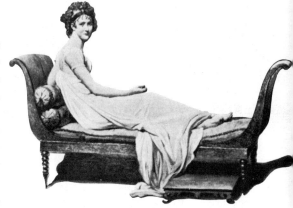

Figure 251. Portrait of Julia Adelaide Recamier *by Jacques Louis David. Mme. Recamier was celebrated for her audacious salon in Paris during the Directoire until after the fall of Napoleon I. She appears here in the typical fashion of her time, wearing an evening dress of light voile with a Grecian style hairdo. Louvre, Paris.*

247

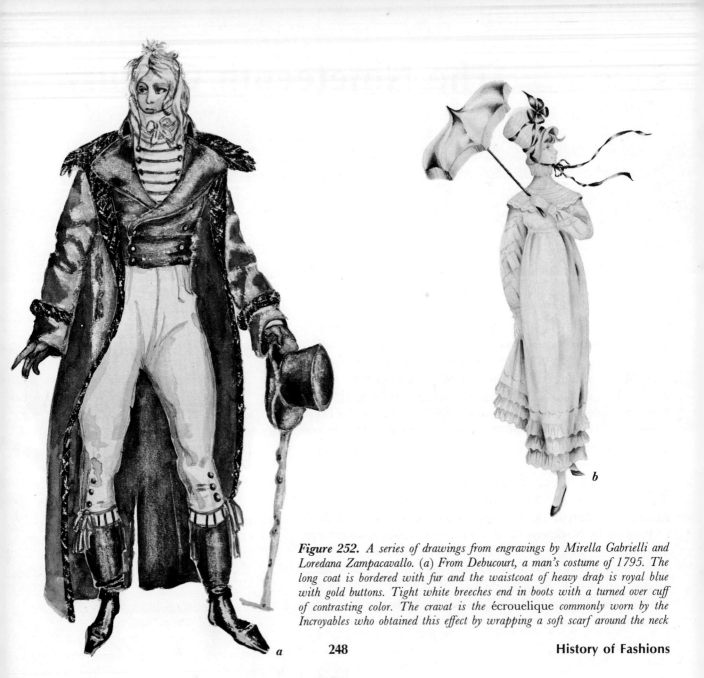

Figure 252. *A series of drawings from engravings by Mirella Gabrielli and Loredana Zampacavallo. (a) From Debucourt, a man's costume of 1795. The long coat is bordered with fur and the waistcoat of heavy drap is royal blue with gold buttons. Tight white breeches end in boots with a turned over cuff of contrasting color. The cravat is the* écrouelique *commonly worn by the Incroyables who obtained this effect by wrapping a soft scarf around the neck*

c   d

and chin, crossing it in back, and tying it in front with a butterfly knot. The hair is done en oreilles de chien. (b) From 1806, an attractive dress in light linen with sleeves, skirt, and collar decorated with cotton lace. Typical is the high crown of the bonnet tied round and round with satin ribbon. (c) Afternoon dress for a Parisian gentleman of 1807 is composed of light knee breeches, dark green frock coat, and lace cravat. The shoes are very light and without heels. (d) A Parisian lady's costume of 1810. The dress is of white mousseline with pleated ruffles enriching the short bodice and the hem of the long, slender skirt. A dark red shawl of embroidered velvet makes a brilliant contrast. (e) "Corriere delle Dame" of 1820 shows this typical spencer jacket in amaranth velvet, decorated and fastened with frogs. It is worn over a light, white dress trimmed with lace volants. The bonnet is trimmed with tiny flowers.

The Nineteenth Century   **249**

e

Figure 252 (continued). (*f*) *A French fashion plate of 1824 shows the first real trousers, ankle length and tapered. Patterned hose, bowed pumps, and the top hat are all typical accessories.* (*g*) *From "Corriere delle Dame" 1832, a sports costume and an afternoon dress. The riding dress consists of a belted dark gray skirt topped by a white shirt with enormous puffed sleeves. A black tie and a top hat trimmed with a large veil complete the costume. The afternoon dress with full skirt and puffed sleeves is worn with a stole of embroidered silk. Both ladies present the wasp waist silhouette.* (*h*) *Two views of evening*

History of Fashions

f

g

dress in lavishly embroidered taffetas. The hair is dressed in the shape of a cockscomb with fanciful ornaments on top and the characteristic curls at the sides of the head. (i) From the "Musée des Familles" of 1866, two evening dresses in taffetas and satin. Worn over the full crinoline, they are trimmed with little roses and precious lace. (j) From the "Moniteur de la Mode" of 1885, two coquettish models wear dresses with tightly fitted bodices and soft skirts capriciously gathered in poufs.

The Nineteenth Century   251

He demanded, however, that his officials wear embroidered costumes and that his servants appear in sumptuous liveries. Above all, he gave a great deal of money for the elegance of the ladies at the Court; and the Empress Josephine, who was a model of sophistication and beauty, received fabulous sums to spend on herself.

The ladies of the court wore long dresses, still in very light fabrics such as mousseline, and delicate, flat slippers, often tied with ribbons at the ankle (Figure 253). In contrast to the lightness of the fabrics and the extreme décolletage, heavy velvet cloaks fell from the high waistline in back and ended in elegant trains. The hair was dressed *à la grecque,* enriched with curls and ribbons.

The Italian Canova portrayed the image of the beautiful ladies of the court, attempting to renew the perfection of Greek sculpture. An outstanding example of his art, conserved in the Borghese Museum in Rome, is the white marble statue of Pauline Bonaparte. Also inspired by antique models of beauty were the great German poet Goethe and the Italian Foscolo.

But all this world dreamed of by Napoleon and created by his artists very soon fell apart. On March 31, 1814, the allied troops entered Paris and Napoleon was unable to save his city. He was banished to Elba and, in the general chaos that followed, thrones and dynasties were swept away. States appeared and disappeared; spectacular new inventions shortened distances and gave the world a new appearance.

In France, with the death of Louis XVIII, the aristocracy was ejected from power; and the bourgeoisie, feeling its new dignity, entered on the stage of the Nineteenth Century—which would be *its* century. The image of Napoleon dissolved, and all Europe seemed to want to rest from the Revolution and from those events which, in a certain sense, continued it. There was a vivid aspiration but without precise outlines,

History of Fashions

Figure 253. Valzer *from "La Belle Assemblée" 1817. The dresses of the young dancers retain the empire waistline but now have more conical skirts. The men wear long-tailed* fracs *with fitted knee breeches. New York Public Library.*

The Nineteenth Century   253

Figure 254. *Portrait of the Italian poet,* Vincenzo Monti, *by Andrea Appiani (1754–1817). Casual elegance is apparent in the softly draped shirt and cravat worn with a velvet-collared jacket. Academy of Fine Arts, Venice.*

History of Fashions

and it became confused with the desire for political and economic freedom. According to these new ideals, a new order was establishing a new society. The French Revolution had greatly influenced other countries, and everywhere similar tendencies signaled a revolution of ideals—that is, a real evolution.

The costume of this epoch created clear lines which were remarkable and still used even today. For several years the empire line, high waistline and dress of pure white, remained in fashion; but it became heavier with the addition of ornaments, in tune with the new taste in fabrics and embroideries. Parasols very often completed the gracious fashions—especially the dress for morning in white cotton, garnished by little ruffles at the hem, on the shoulders, and sleeves. The necklines were very high, finished with ruffles; also worn were special coiffes decorated with ribbons (see Figures 252b and d).

Light corsets returned to make the brief bodice rigid. And short jackets, in velvet or broadcloth, were in fashion; called the *spencer*, they derived from men's fashions (see Figure 252e). The skirt, conical and rigid but not wide, left the ankle uncovered and usually ended with padded decorations twisted in spirals and ennobled with little roses.

For men the fashionable color was blue. The shoes had a little heel, and the trousers were definitely narrow and long (see Figure 252f). The "top hat" replaced the Napoleonic hat and, for about ten years, the essential lines did not change.

Together with David, Manageot and Appiani must be considered masters of the Neo-Classic school of painting. This vivacious trio was able to renew the Neo-Classic theatrical costume which for a certain time had been contained within the narrow limits of a cold imitation of antiquity (Figure 254).

Jean Auguste Dominique Ingres left refined portraits in delicate colors where the tenuous expressions seem conceived in a sort of Raphaelite style, but which he composed by putting color and expression second to the line itself. Ingres was David's best pupil and a perfect draftsman (Plate 9).

Little by little, the waistline in women's dresses went back to its natural place, and the sleeves became puffed like balloons. Imperceptibly but decidedly, the new line of the Romantic epoch appeared (see Figure 252g). The romantic ladies coveted the wasp-waisted look, and over the rich skirt they wore a belt like a corset to squeeze the waistline. For their dresses, they used mostly taffetas, velvet, and audacious embroideries and colors.

The boa of fur became a very common accessory, and jewels and decorations were inspired by the pinnacles of Gothic architecture, which was rapidly spreading through the general taste in many different motifs. In the Italian magazine *Corriere delle Dame,* 1832, it is possible to see typical dresses of the period and some amusing and typical hairdos.

The evening dress for young ladies very often had décolletages formed by crossed bands of ruffles and decorations of colored velvet appliquéd in relief. The hairdressing, in the form of a cockscomb, soared high above the small curls clustered at the temples (see Figures 252h and i).

At the time of the wasp waist, men also wore a corset to make their waists thinner under the frock. With padded sleeves, jabot, and narrow pants showing decorated hose, they wore light slippers with a bow at the toe (see Figure 252f). Their preferred colors were cypress green, black, violet, and blue. The waistcoat was now called a *gilet,* deriving its name from Gilles, a character of the French popular theater, who wore a jacket without sleeves. The gilet was made of broadcloth or of silk with colored flowers.

Romanticism influenced costume, furniture, architecture, the arts, and literature (Figure 255). Private salons of famous

Figure 255. Portrait of a Young Lady *by Michelangelo Grigoletti (1801–1879). The diadem set oddly askew and the sheer blouse of Brussels lace are characteristic of the new romantic taste. Galleria Nazionale d'Arte Moderna, Rome.*

ladies became the new centers at which many artists, such as Lamartine, de Musset, Balzac, and Byron found success and fame.

The new theatrical costume sought to give the psychological content of the character. In other words, if Neo-Classicism regarded the spectacle as a problem of historical reconstruction, now the research was for a new kind of period-style characterization and was entrusted to the costume designer. The houses of costume, controlled by the *costumiste,* rose to the importance of autonomous industries which turned out costumes in series. But, because the theatrical spectacle is too highly important and artistic to accept costumes made on a production line, this type of organization damaged the taste in dramatic art.

The Nineteenth Century 257

After 1840, with the creation of banks and the affirmation of a money aristocracy, all the principles of elegance appeared confused in an anxious search for certain majestic decorations, which determined the decline of taste in manners and costume. In fact, fashion and custom always operate together in history and civilization.

Even as Romanticism entered its period of decline, a new current, that of Realism, was born. There is an evident relationship between the spirit of the Nineteenth Century and realistic art. The romantic artists, oppressed by the Machine Age, had sought escape in an imaginary world; the realists found that type of evasion too easy and believed that art could be made to comply with scientific and industrial progress.

Meanwhile in Europe the Industrial Revolution erupted, bringing with it the new demands of the working classes. In art, painters began to introduce the world of farmers and workers, and society was exposed to the colorful bad taste of the *mondaines*. There was not really a style in the general sense; rather, a meaningless imitation of other styles developed. And all was falsely pompous.

Honoré Daumier was the most celebrated artist of Realism; Daumier was, above all, an onlooker who was able to give to the object of his reflections a formidable strength. He left extraordinarily plastic designs, many representing political parodies and others burlesquing the fashions of that time (Figure 256).

A spirited painter of costume was Edouard Beaumont who collaborated with newspapers and magazines such as *Le Moniteur*, one of the most important fashion magazines of the century. In Paris Beaumont founded the French Society of Watercolor Painters (Figure 257).

After 1850, men's trousers were tight-fitting, longer, and they were striped or in large checks; almost always they were made of fabrics different from the jacket. Also *this* was a period

History of Fashions

Figure 256. A humorous lithograph by Honoré Daumier (1808–1879) satirizes the legal profession. The seated man, wearing striped long trousers, shows the fashion popular after mid-century; the attorney wears the characteristic black robe and white plastron. Cappelli Collection.

Figure 257. Les Jolies Femmes de Paris, 1858, by Edouard Beaumont. This lithograph clearly illustrates the men's style of wearing checkered trousers with a solid colored redingote.. The monocle and top hat are typical accessories. Cappelli Collection.

Figure 258. *This gravure humorously illustrates the disapproval by the clergy of coquettish ladies wearing over-sized crinolines in church. Author's collection; Cappelli Collection.*

of intensive gallantry; men were very concerned with their elegance and observed the world through a monocle. Their jackets were long, in the redingote line, and ended just above the knee. These had velvet collars and were created in solid colors that complemented their patterned trousers. The men wore their hair rather long and they sported full sidewhiskers which sometimes met at the chin to form a beard.

The ladies adopted a bell-shaped cloak, and jackets inspired by the Russian costume were closed by frogs. Their coiffures, which had become very simple, were gracefully knotted, originating the well-known chignon. In this period the imagination of the women resulted in a great fantasy of coiffe-shaped hats for which precious laces and light fabrics were selected. They were completed by refined, sophisticated decorations of ribbons and flowers. The most elaborate were called *chapeaux*

à *bavolet* and were made with plumes of feathers. Some of these hats, smaller and simpler and sometimes finished with a narrow ruffle, derived from the bonnet—originally a small cap without a brim.

At the court of Napoleon III, the couturières Palmire and Vignon translated the romantic taste of the Spanish Empress with new experiments; and thus the *crinoline* was born as a new kind of reinforcement for the feminine skirts (Figure 258). The crinoline began by being cone shaped, the fabric stiffened with horse hair. Later, the Englishman Thompson invented the cage of iron, and still later, the French Delirac succeeded in making it lighter and flexible (Figure 259).

Over that armor the ladies wore several skirts in silk, mousseline, and often dentelle. The top one was generally delicately decorated with satin ribbons, ruches, and flowers—a gracious

Figure 259. Skating in Central Park by Winslow Homer (1836–1910) announces the beginning of America's leadership in female emancipation. These audacious American couples are skating in crinoline and top hat! City Art Museum, St. Louis; Eliza McMillan Fund.

The Nineteenth Century   261

expression of femininity and coquettry. For ten years the crinoline was very popular in all categories of feminine dress. But, though it could present a delightful picture at court balls and evening functions of the aristocracy, it became merely grotesque when used by the bourgeoisie; and, really, it clashed with their way of life.

After 1860 the crinoline changed and appeared puffed up just in the back of the skirt; later, little by little, it would disappear. That new style, the half-crinoline skirt, was well accepted everywhere and found elegant interpretations. The fashion was completed by fine shawls, often in dentelle. The shawl, which came into fashion at the end of the Eighteenth Century, was of Oriental origin. Indian designs, which were very popular, were reproduced in embroidery on fine fabrics; later, the same Kashmir styles were transformed into woven materials by French industries and widely distributed. After Napoleon's campaign in Egypt, the fabric of the turbans of the ancient Mameluks was utilized even for dresses by the ladies.

The Russian costume at that time used motifs of the apron, dark colors, and shawls in black wool with long fringe; and embroidered in one corner of the shawl was a bunch of red and pink roses. The women covered their heads with narrow scarves, often in antique-white dentelle, and wore red coral brooches and earrings (see Figure 294b).

Gustave Courbet was the master of the Realists; he sought to establish relationships between the political, socialist principles of Proudhon with his own convictions and concepts of painting (Figure 260). But about 1860, Courbet came into contact with Claude Monet and Eugene Boudin, and thus was born Impressionism, which was destined to produce many

The Nineteenth Century 263

Figure 261. Ladies in the Garden *by Claude Monet (1840–1926) displays a delightful ensemble of the finest fashion models of the time. Light dresses in dotted white mousseline, striped taffetas, and delicately embroidered voile are worn over the half-crinoline, endowing the ladies with a gracious and most feminine appearance. Louvre, Paris.*

great painters. Those artists, so concerned with the reflections of light and color, often coupled to the beauty of nature the grace of current fashions and many exquisite paintings of costume resulted (Figure 261).

Edouard Manet never belonged to the Impressionist group but seemed, rather, to be a precursor of it. One might say that he was an historical painter, so well did he describe the society and costume of his time. Also atypical of the Impres-

Figure 265. A pen drawing by Renoir illustrates a street ensemble of heavily pleated skirt and astrakhan jacket. The lady wears a charming little hat composed of *voilette* and flowers and she buries her hands in a sable muff. Authorization SPADEM, by the French Reproduction Rights, Inc. New York.

In 1869 Queen Victoria and the Princess Metternich rejected the crinoline and introduced new feminine styles by draping the skirt into the *tournure,* creating a line not so far from the natural proportions of the figure when seen from the front. But seen in profile, it presented a very surprising silhouette because the overskirt, always present in the robe tournure, created monumental drapings in the rear (Figure 263). That style reached its most amusing exaggeration in 1886 with the famous *tournure strapontin.* With this rich line the ladies preferred little hats, called *capotes,* usually made with ribbons and small feathers. For the coiffure, the hair was gathered on the crown of the head and sometimes fell in one or more long curls on the neck.

The sleeves, which were still puffed at the elbow during the crinoline period, now fell loose and bell-shaped, ending in refinements of volants in taffetas or dentelle.

During the Romantic era, flat slippers tied around the ankles with ribbons remained in style, but with the tournure the shoes acquired small heels. In the last years of the Nineteenth Century, the ladies adopted close-fitting, buttoned boots in fine kidskin with a small heel.

After 1870 the ladies again composed their long skirts with an evident fullness formed by pleats and with a sort of wraparound overskirt which ended behind in soft, large knots. This was called the *pouf,* and it was supported by a little cushion shaped in the same way as the *faux cul* of a century earlier (Figures 264, 265). It was a coquettish addition to the tournure. It is very amusing to see that some umbrellas were

Figure 266. *These two fashion models of the 1870's show interesting variations of the tournure, which was formed by a crinoline reduced in size but protruding in back to form a bustle; this created a profile similar to that of the* faux cul *of a century earlier. This style is revived in 1885 and finds its most grotesque interpretation in the* tournure strapontin. *Engraving from author's collection.*

created with the same silhouette to accompany the pouf. Sober colors, minute embroideries, small hats, little muffs, and the most charming parasols of all epochs were in fashion. The skirts, so rich behind, contrasted with the simple jackets which followed the natural line of the figure (Figure 266).

Men's fashions did not change, but became simplified with the fall of Napoleon III and the taste for exhibitionism. European men's fashions began to be guided by England, where useful innovations in children's styles also were created.

The Prince of Wales suggested refined details to the gentlemen: gilets in white *piqué,* and long, narrow trousers with footstraps, which had sometimes appeared in the 1850's. During the first half of the century, designs for men's fashions were inspired by the famous English dandy George Brummel, who had stressed an elegance which must not be apparent. He had been the favorite of the Prince of Wales (subsequently George IV) and was considered a supreme model for the English aristocracy.

The redingote was now adopted as the most elegant and commonly used jacket, and it was worn with or without a cloak. In addition, men wore short jackets and, for evening, the frock coat. The rabat, which in the Seventeenth Century was the square collar, now became a cravat.

From 1870 Europe saw the beginning of the *Belle Epoque.* It was a time when the bourgeoisie loved to indulge in carefree mirth without thinking of the reason behind the laughter. But the sense of respectability, typically bourgeois, provided a brake to this gaiety and a curb to brilliance.

In the *café-chantants* moved a world of ephemeral ambitions and glories. A joie de vivre but not-always-genuine merriment, a world and a custom identified the café-chantants with the Belle Epoque (Figure 267). For the origin of the café-chantants, before the café-concert, it is impossible to precisely

History of Fashions

Figure 267. Free interpretation of the famous Belle Otero, who became a symbol of the "Belle Epoque." Drawing by Gabrielli, author's collection.

Figure 269. In Au Moulin Rouge *Henri Toulouse-Lautrec (1864–1901) recreates the atmosphere of that famous café. Courtesy of The Art Institute, Chicago; Helen Birch Bartlett Memorial Collection.*

Figure 268. A photograph of La Goulue, the celebrated entertainer and dancer of the Moulin Rouge, immortalized by Toulouse-Lautrec. From "La Penultima Moda," Alfredo Panzini, Ed. Cremonese.

establish the date and the country. Certainly in London and, above all, in Paris this type of salon and show developed. The most famous was that called "Au Moulin Rouge" in Paris, immortalized by Henri Toulouse-Lautrec, who occupied a very important place in the society and in the art of his epoch (Figures 268, 269).

About 1875 musical comedy was born as a genre of brilliant spectacle wherein story, songs, and dance were mixed. It developed in Europe and in the United States, but it was tied primarily to the names of Offenbach and Strauss. Vienna, in the Nineteenth Century, was the cultural center for many people from many countries. The bourgeoisie demanded different kinds of amusements, and Strauss fascinated the new society by his waltzes, representing all that in Vienna was lovely and merry.

Meanwhile, overcoming the bizarre theatrical styles and symbolizing the special character of the new spectacles, the costume followed its evolution. In the last years of the Nineteenth Century, the *tailleur* and the *princesse* appeared. The *tailleur* positively initiated its ascent to determine from then on one of the most significant lines of elegance (Figure 270).

Figure 270. After 1880 the dress lost its superfluous reinforcements. A new long corset, reaching to the hips, came into fashion and created a tall, slender silhouette very flat in front. Volants and fringes enriched this simpler style. The embroidered velvet cape and dolman were the most popular wraps. Engraving from author's collection.

Figure 271. *By the last years of the century the line of ladies' dresses had become much simpler. This photograph illustrates some features characteristic of the 1890's: fitted sleeves puffed at the shoulder, high-boned collar, ample bosom exaggerated by ruffles; tiny waist, graceful bell-shaped skirt. From "La Penultima Moda," Alfredo Panzini, Cremonese.*

Figure 272. *In America the bicycling costume became a necessity for the more emancipated ladies. This young woman wears a skirt that appears to be divided into bloomers, a tailored shirt, and a short jacket with sleeves puffed above the elbow. Her hat and shoes are quite sensible. Photograph from author's collection.*

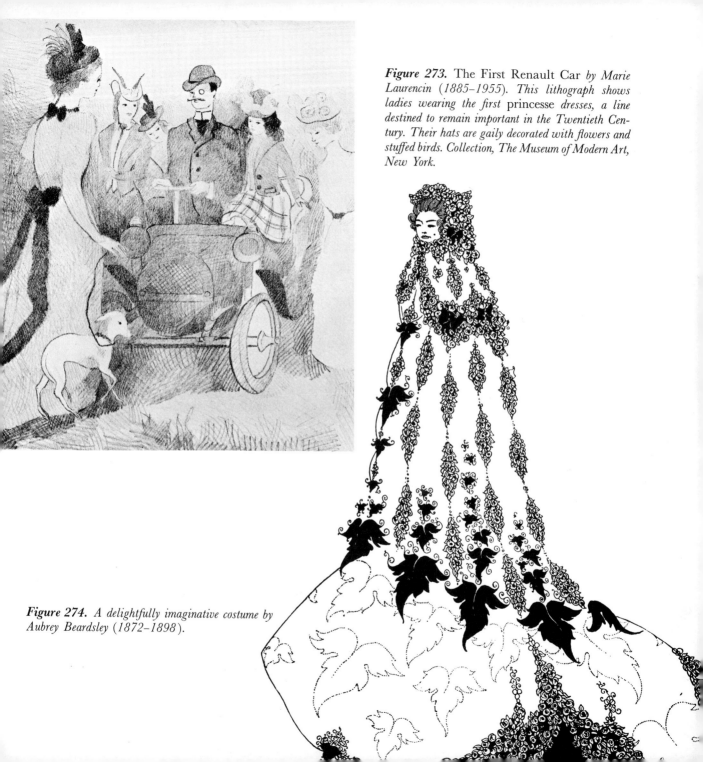

Figure 273. The First Renault Car *by Marie Laurencin (1885–1955). This lithograph shows ladies wearing the first* princesse *dresses, a line destined to remain important in the Twentieth Century. Their hats are gaily decorated with flowers and stuffed birds. Collection, The Museum of Modern Art, New York.*

Figure 274. *A delightfully imaginative costume by Aubrey Beardsley (1872–1898).*

At the same time, the pouf was loosened into a simple, softly flared skirt, and sleeves again became elaborated. At the end of this century, the ladies adopted unexpected sleeves coming from monumental shoulders, à volants, and straw hats with flowers and birds. And the hairdos began to announce the new styles of the twentieth century (Figure 271).

Liberalism arrived on the scene and invaded literature, politics, and society. America introduced a new sense of independence in education to European society, and women began to fight for their emancipation. Movement, sport, the bicycle, made it necessary for women to adopt suitable dress (Figures 272, 273).

At this point, we must mention Aubrey Beardsley who was a talented graphic artist and also a designer of costume. He was a *fin de siècle* painter who scandalized England, but remains the finest expression of the English *Art Nouveau*. A child prodigy, he had but a brief life and did not live to see the century that he foresaw and anticipated; an age in which he has been highly regarded and frequently interpreted. He saw a black and white world, absurd and precise, mysteriously blooming with stylized flowers and personalities, sly but elegant, where color was unknown (Figure 274).

Meanwhile, Paul Gauguin, putting color before design, created modern color—a symbolic and decorative unity in which the last flight of Romanticism found its expression (Plate 10).

The Twentieth Century

In the beginning of the Twentieth Century, the Expressionists stated that they did not paint in the name of art, but in the name of humanity. The Expressionists renounced "art for art's sake," which had been a basic idea of Impressionism, and, believing art less important than strength of expression, they dedicated themselves to developing this particular message.

The Twentieth Century, in fact, is the century of expressionism, activism, dynamism, and new technology. In every field Expressionism signifies an art that expresses with exasperated intensity the many different human feelings, inspirations, deceptions, and passions of the modern world.

In the fields of philosophy, politics, and sociology, there were many protests against the mechanization of modern life; in opposition to it, the new artists started from intuition and visualized an immaterial universe overcoming reality. There was a sort of internal tension to oppose the traditions, disciplines, and all that was conventional.

275

Figure 275. *A scene showing the ambience and costumes of the* café-chantant.

For the first decade of this century, on the stage of the café-chantants the "can-can" dancers were still wearing rich skirts, à volants, in dramatic colors; black stockings with visible, sophisticated garters, and long ostrich boas (Figure 275). Meanwhile, fine ladies adopted long dresses, often in chantilly lace, with tight-fitting sleeves, soft hairdos, and parasols with long handles and flounces of silk.

At that time, the basics in ladies' costumes were the tailleur and the princesse, which really were born in the last lines and years of the Nineteenth Century. The skirts were still long, to the floor, and a little flared; the sleeves, close-fitting to the elbow, ended in volants or in puffed cuffs. The most used fabrics were the voiles in silk and cotton with appliquéd decorations in lace. The bodices were often closed at the neck by a lightly boned band, and the front was enriched by some motifs of bolero or by very delicate jabots (Figure 276).

Long necklaces were in fashion, long strings of pearls, pink corals, amber, or jade. The silhouette was very often completed by enormous feathered hats, and sometimes dresses had a brief train (Figure 277).

Figure 276. *A lovely dress in voile banded with lace from 1902. At the beginning of this century skirts flared at the hem; the shoulders were narrow, but the sleeves were full and soft, and were often closed at the wrist by a snug, buttoned cuff. The soft, nest-shaped hairdos usually had a small bun in the center. From the "Penultima Moda," A. Panzini, Cremonese.*

Figure 277. *A princesse line in chantilly lace from 1909. The huge, broad-brimmed hat complements the very straight, high-necked dress. From "La Penultima Moda," A. Panzini, Cremonese.*

Figure 279. A tennis dress of 1905 is in white linen, decorated with dainty, pale blue embroidery. Library of Accademia Italiana di Costume, Rome.

Figure 278. A morning costume of 1903, composed of a flared and belted dark skirt worn with a finely pleated crêpe blouse. A black butterfly tie decorates the high starched collar; and a flat straw hat, imitating men's styles, completes the fashion. From "La Penultima Moda," A. Panzini, Cremonese.

Lovely blouses were in fashion too; generally they were made of light silk or cotton and adorned with varied embroideries and volants. They were often worn with dark-colored skirts and rigid straw hats, covered with stylized flowers and waxed ribbons (Figures 278, 279).

Elegantly, Boldini painted exquisite portraits of beautiful ladies of the European aristocracy, with deep décolletages full of roses and bits of black velvet around the swanlike neck (Figure 280).

At the same time, men wore stiff collars and cuffs, black ties à l'artiste, or long ties with precious tiepins; striped trousers, and still the redingote (Figure 281). Loden, a soft wool cloth, was used to make a special coat called macfarlane, a large coat without sleeves and with a long pèlerine.

History of Fashions

Figure 281. In his portrait of Count Robert de Montesquieu, *Boldini shows the elegant man of fashion wearing, still, the redingote with silk lapels. His necktie* à l'artiste, *light gloves, and ebony cane are favorite accessories. Musée National d'Art Moderne, Paris.*

Figure 280. This portrait of Mlle. Lanthelme *by Giovanni Boldini (1842–1931), freely sketched, is significantly illustrative of the fashion of his time. Galleria Nazionale d'Arte Moderna, Rome.*

Figure 282. *Changing silhouettes of the second decade of the Twentieth Century. (a) A tailleur of 1911 with portfolio skirt and long jacket. The blouse has a lace jabot for softness, and the huge hat is covered with panaches. (b) In 1914, following the ridiculous style of the* entrave, *skirts were arranged to resemble Turkish trousers, exhibiting a strange, Oriental influence. (c) Unexpectedly, in 1915, skirts became much shorter and wider—decidedly bell-shaped—revealing ankle-high, exquisitely feminine boots. (d) A typical example of the "spindle" line: a soft blousant coat, in dark green broadcloth is trimmed with black fox fur and decorated with black silk* passementerie. *From "La Penultima Moda," A. Panzini, Cremonese.*

Figure 283. In 1912, there was a brief return to the empire waistline and light, delicate fabrics. From "La Penultima Moda," A. Panzini, Cremonese.

Figure 284. A dress en entrave *from 1912. This absurdly amusing style lasted just one year, but it influenced fashion by narrowing skirts at the hemline, creating the "hobble" effect. From "La Penultima Moda" by A. Panzini, Cremonese.*

While men's fashions did not change for many years, women's costume seems to have been extraordinarily capricious and changed many different lines within a few years (Figures 282a–d). In 1912 there was a sudden, very brief return to the empire waistline, to which was added the surprising style of the *entrave,* an unreasonably placed ribbon which constricted the skirt under the knees, impeding movement (Figures 283, 284). After only one year, skirts were arranged in the manner of turkish trousers, with which courageous ladies wore tall *aigrettes* on the head, supported by tiny hats or by simple hairdos.

In 1915, waistlines came back to the natural place and were emphasized by tight-fitting bodices, in contrast with the bell-shaped basques. Skirts, sensibly shorter, were also bell shaped and were complemented by elegant, ankle-length boots in kidskin.

The Twentieth Century   **281**

Simultaneously, men inaugurated the complete suit in black and white checked fabrics. They carried malacca canes and wore straw hats and merry, butterfly-style neckties (Figure 285a).

In about 1918, feminine fashions began to create acceptable styles which, little by little, produced the new, spindle-shaped silhouette with long, elegant, blousant bodices, new softness, and ample, dramatic capes adorned with fur—especially sable, mole, or black fox.

Hair was worn shorter at the sides and was arranged behind in simple, small chignons. But the ladies who adopted those styles, apparently so sober and soft, also felt a wistful desire to appear eccentric, and they used audacious decorations in contrasting lines and colors.

These were the years following the First World War, and the natural reaction of the people was to want to have fun. At that time a restless humanity was anxious to create something new and relevant to disperse old griefs. In every field there was crisis and agitation, and the dramatic feeling of the time found desperate and intense expressions in all the artistic currents: pictorial, literary, musical, and cultural in general. The *Novecento* found, perhaps, its culmination in those years after the war; a widespread sense of freedom encouraged exploration but often led to errors of taste in art and costume.

Cubism, which had its beginnings before the war, was enriched after 1912 when Picasso and Braque introduced the first form of collage—little pieces of paper or cloth, splinters of glass, and colored sand. The synthetic phase of Cubism started in 1913 and this movement broke the last links with tradition, creating a special, plastic, autonomous language. With a more dynamic character, Futurism developed in Italy. It conceived visual impressions of motion and used abstract, geometric fragments of color to reveal a world seen through

Figure 285. (a) Men's fashions after 1916 caricatured by the Spanish designer, Deribas. (b) The great German Expressionist, Ernst Ludwig Kirchner, satirizes women's styles. Author's collection.

Figure 286. A costume study in the Futuristic manner for "Altitudes," a production of the Teatro Plastico Depero (1918). Palazzo Odescalchi, Rome.

a kaleidoscope. The convincing value of the Futurist experiences consisted in their adaptation of pictorial expressions to the forms of modern life. Its influence also moved efficaciously into theatrical interpretations of costume and set (Figure 286).

To excite, to provoke emotion, artists ignored harmony, which then became difficult to maintain. That passionate search for dramatic effect left fantasy absolutely free to put together the most varied images: geometric figures, curved and straight lines, brushstrokes of color with infinite possibilities of variation. The artistic movement which particularly expressed this difficult *impasse* was Surrealism; it found its inspiration in an exploration of the subconscious mind and the ever-new world of "tomorrow." That same Surrealism had provoked personal reactions in every artist and some of them, feeling secret moving forces—the so-called "metaphysical anguish"—created new motifs of expression. The leading exponents of that style were Giorgio de Chirico, Giorgio Morandi, Joan Miró, André Masson, Max Ernst, and later, Salvador Dali made his own very personal contribution.

The art of Picasso is an art of protest, of opposition, of combat for man's liberty. More than any other artist, Picasso validly represents the spirit of the Twentieth Century and, like his own century, he has consistently ignored traditional rules in the construction of his works; instead of coherence, there is always surprise.

In drama Gabriele d'Annunzio, dramatic author and poet, dreamed of a theater of poesy free and far from commercial speculations. Eleonora Duse, the inspired actress, brought with her voice—which was like a song—a new spirit of faith to the European and transoceanic crowds. The theatrical costume for her was a special costume, perfectly fitting to the personages she portrayed, but always designed in simple, pure outlines (Figure 287). With a mystic experience she closed her

Figure 287. Eleonora Duse, the inspired Italian actress, in the role of Silvia Settana in "La Gioconda" by Gabriele d'Annunzio.

b

a

Figure 288. Two evening dresses of the "twenties:" (a) A silhouette of 1922 with streamers of fabric trailing on the ground. Author's collection. (b) A perfect model of high fashion by Chanel, 1925; of pink lace, it is arranged in four tiers and complemented with an ostrich feather fan. The mannequin shows the popular new haircut, the "boyish bob." Museum of Fine Arts, Boston; gift of Mrs. Francis B. Lothrop and Mrs. George L. Batchelder.

great career in New York City, reciting *Porta Chiusa* by Marco Praga. Returning to Italy, she died very soon in the gentle solitude of Asolo, near Venice.

Naturally, at that time, all types of spectacles were greatly appreciated. The singers and *soubrettes* found traditional enthusiasm and introduced to the private salons the new dances, new taste, beliefs, and fashions born in America. And the attitudes deriving from the various forms of art, a modernism along with a decadence, presented an interesting populace.

The costume as clothing was also very interesting. Many motifs, deriving from various exotic influences, were evident; but America overwhelmed the uncertain masses and its influence was to predominate for a decade.

In fact, after 1920, we see the costume deeply influenced by the life and manners of the United States. Hairstyles became decidedly shorter; the naked neck appeared longer, and women played nervously with their necklaces, flourishing long, slender cigarette holders. This was the beginning of the courageous modern woman: affected but seductive, superficial but amusing; exhibiting pink or white silk stockings, small shoes with straps and high heels, fearless drapings, flounces of silk or swan feathers, and dresses of crêpe-satin in black, white, pink, or beige (Figure 288).

The introduction of jazz was an important phenomenon in the history of music. In the beginning it seemed to be a simple expression of Negro spirituals and Negro–American folklore. But later it became a universal art which, while belonging above all to the big American cities, was widespread through all countries of the world—especially appreciated and interpreted in Europe. And if we wish to determine its place in contemporary Occidental civilization, we can say that it represented a sort of reaction to the extreme individualism of Western art and a desire to return to simple forms. Jazz is

Figure 289. A costume study for "The New York Mulatto" in the ballet, "The New Babel," a 1930 New York production of the Teatro Plastico Depero.

a genre of modern music which is tied to the gesture and thus it contains the basics of a spectacle. In a certain sense, too, it implies a special costume (Figure 289).

In 1925 skirts were extremely shortened and opened with *godets,* outwardly resembling petals of flowers. Sometimes the short skirts were made from a very long fringe falling from the low waistline.

Women wore tight, close-fitting hats, decorated by a large flower or cockade, or huge bows. Décolletages were very deep in the back and extra lengths of cloth floated from them. Very often, long and short godets circled the hem of the dress. Sashes or ribbons marked and bound the hips. And cloaks had fluffy collars in white or blue fox; sometimes the collar was made of frilled fabrics in the rocaille style. The Charleston shook skirts, hair, legs, and ideas of the lean "crisis" girls, thin as rails (Figure 290).

All that confusion had to produce a natural reaction, which arrived very soon and laid to rest the fantasies. By 1930, in fact, the movies disclosed new incarnations of the eternal femininity: two different types of beauty, the great Greta Garbo

History of Fashions

Figure 290. Brunetta, well known Italian designer, catches the spirit of 1926; the impertinence of these ladies is described in her words:

"Endlessly, they rise above things,
They don't look where they go,
But it does not matter—
They are so fashionable."

By courtesy of the artist.

Figure 291. *Greta Garbo represents the new feminine ideal of independence in her adoption of masculine tailleurs, soft, crêpe blouses, and deep* cloches.

and the "vamp with class" Marlene Dietrich, subtly showed
an ideal, fulfilled woman, simple in appearance, yet fascinating and mysterious. Soft *cloches* in felt shaded their expressions,
and they adopted a masculine-looking tailleur with long
jacket, hiding the natural curves. Their slender bodies were
revealed only when they wore light, long, wrapped princesses
in silk crêpe, slanted in bias cuts (Figure 291).

With the woman of the "thirties," and with the recognized
affirmation of her type, the history of costume arrived at a
very important plateau where it rested for many years. In
fact, the style never really departed completely because even
recently it appears in some modern lines as a nostalgia for
that smooth grace.

After 1930 there were only some brief, fleeting styles, proposed without conviction and rapidly terminated. Little by
little, fabrics began to acquire more importance than the lines;
some were inspired by costumes of the past, others by exotic
fashions. But really, for twenty years there were styles which
certainly cannot become "costume." Nothing new was created,
not one idea was enduring enough to determine a line of
costume.

In 1947, however, after the Second World War, pushed by
Marcel Boussac, the famous tycoon of the textile industry,
Christian Dior created the "New Look." He reinterpreted the
line of 1915—short, tight jackets with basque and bell-shaped
skirts—making the richer, longer skirts with many yards of
fabric! So the industry sold fabrics in large quantities after
the general standstill of the war years. But the "New Look"
was anachronistic and anti-economical after the deprivations
of such a war; so it had a very brief life and was remarkable
only as an economic fact. Chiefly, it made officially and universally known the necessary collaboration between industry
and high fashion—a fact that constitutes the modern concept
for fashion production.

Then, the first interesting line that created a *silhouette* and had universal appeal was designed by Cristobal Balenciaga in 1953 (Figure 292). In fact, it was adopted later by all the great contemporary designers as a point of departure. That feminine type—earlier created in art by Amedeo Modigliani and now consigned to history—immediatedly understood and adopted, dressed and adapted to the exigencies of fashion, remains to symbolize a long period of costume. Since 1953 all the modern creative minds have been inspired by that same silhouette, using endless, different motifs but never abandoning it or going too far from it.

International communication forced art to eliminate national characteristic in favor of visual form; no longer were ethnic qualities to determine the nature of a work of art. When art had been essentially figurative, it was possible to ask, to divine, to identify the images presented by the artists; they revealed some national characteristic, taste, or mentality which, perhaps, the artist had sought to express. The principle of abstraction, on the contrary, eliminates the possibility of seeking traditional signs which, in fact, no longer exist. So, we admit that abstractionism represents a world—modern and international—unified in the common effort for progress.

The contemporary world of abstraction in art flows from two diverse sources: the French *intellectualism* of Picasso and Braque and the *emotionalism* of the German Expressionists, all enriched by the romantic Russian lyricism. These apparently opposite directions in art came together after the Second World War and developed the dynamic movement of Abstract Expressionism. And it stimulated many latent artists. Perhaps some tried it as something to be easily mastered, but later they appreciated it deeply and needed to learn. Very often they were inspired by Japanese and Chinese painting, which was abstract but intellectual.

Figure 292. Typical example of the tunic line created by Cristobal Balenciaga in 1953. This line started a new, enduring epoch of costume and looks as contemporary today as it did seventeen years ago! Author's collection.

Figure 293. *A fabric design by Rosana Pistolese inspired by Japanese painting; it was created for the Fontana Sisters' 1963 collection. Author's collection.*

a

Abstract designs for fabrics rapidly came into fashion, and they appeared in the finest collections of French and Italian couture; almost all were printed in the Italian silk factories of Como (Figure 293; Plates 11, 12, 13). Even Giulio Turcato, well-known Italian painter, designed scarves and fabrics for high fashion.

A new taste and, therefore, a new costume feverishly prepared the way for new industries. From the time of the Renaissance, fashion had been regarded as possessing definite economic possibilities; but after the Second World War, it became one of the most promising sources for new industries anxious to launch it. With the industrialization of fashion came advertising, and then the profession of specialist in public relations—first in the United States, later in all of Europe. The period after the war determined in many countries simultaneous and parallel intentions and tendencies in science, art, custom, and costume (Figures 294a–d).

Figure 294. *Costume for the theater, films, and television by contemporary Italian designers. (a) Costume for Ava Gardner in Henry Koster's film, "The Naked Maja," by Dario Cecchi. (b) A Russian costume of 1876 designed by Rosana Pistolese for Grushenka in the "Brothers Karamazov." Teatro della Cometa, 1960, Rome. (c) A recreation of the fashion of 1913–1914 by Maurizio Monteverde for the theater. (d) A charleston costume for the "Nouvelle Eve," a television production. All from author's collection.*

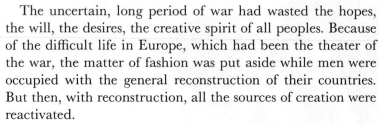

a

The uncertain, long period of war had wasted the hopes, the will, the desires, the creative spirit of all peoples. Because of the difficult life in Europe, which had been the theater of the war, the matter of fashion was put aside while men were occupied with the general reconstruction of their countries. But then, with reconstruction, all the sources of creation were reactivated.

Ladies of the aristocracy created the first *boutiques*—mostly in Italy where the ancient tradition of Italian elegance assisted them. And the boutiques quickly acquired a character of authentic chic which, in a short time, was to make that particular kind of clothing famous and typically Italian.

The big industrial nations, which were soon able to demonstrate the renewal of their activity, seemed oriented toward a *practical* taste in fashions for a modern, free world matured by war. For that reason Italian creation, genuinely original, achieved a great success and unconsciously became engaged in a competition with French fashion. At that moment, however, Italian designers did not consider the possibility of creating "high fashion;" it was rather the triumph of the boutique, which suggested clothing at moderate prices, easy to wear, colorful, and graceful (Plates 14, 15).

It is now generally recognized that today's fashions are created primarily in France and in Italy, where buyers from the whole world convene twice a year to buy and, later, to reproduce the latest models (Figures 295a–c; 296a, b). We can see that Italy and France dominate fashion in this century, but we must add that this endless creativity draws nourish-

Figure 295. *International fashion, 1966–1967. (a) Palazzo pajamas by F. Forquet in a Taroni fabric of silk printed in yellow, orange, and green. (b) Hostess pajamas in black silk chiffon-jersey with black silk Venetian fringe. Designed by Rosana Pistolese for the Collection Oleg Cassini Italia, 1966. (c) In lacquer-red jersey, this evening dress by Biki was inspired by the Indian sari. 1967. Courtesy of the designer.*

b

c

 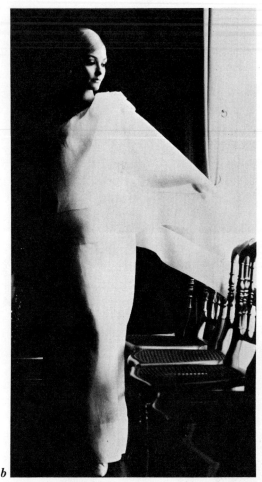

Figure 296. *Two evening dresses in the Christian Dior 1967 collection: (a) pale pink shantung from Lajoinie is garnished with a cascade of flowers down one sleeve; (b) white organdy from Brivet. Both coiffures are by Alexandre, Paris. Photographs by Studio Jean-Paulcade. Courtesy of the designer.*

ment from the enormous organization for mass production which has been wonderfully developed first in the United States, then in Germany, Japan, and England.

England, which in its earlier appearances in the historical development of costume always contributed moderate innovations, recently presented exaggerated interpretations of contemporary society.

The United States, because of its vastness and ultramodern technical establishment, absorbs the major part of the designers' efforts. And this effort, at present, is very important because fashion activities embrace a large number of commercial interests operating in its production and distribution. In a world of work which today involves so many international interests, casual improvisation cannot be authorized or tolerated. All the civilized countries now feel a need to have people thoroughly prepared in a field which concerns all the life of man, from art to science.

The relations between man and the universe (which has lost its reassuring stability) can be modified not only by science, but above all by inspiration of the arts. Light, traveling through space and arriving in our atmosphere, produces colors in all their varieties. Throughout the centuries men and women have felt the mysterious presence of color and desired to find its essence. The color of precious stones seems to be the *real* essence of color and, looking at them, we have the sensation of not being able to distinguish material limits. Color suggests fantastic images and inspires motifs of decoration because we would like to imprison it, to frame it, to formalize its beauty.

Even the ancients attributed magical qualities to color and they believed, also, that because of their colors, precious stones, being part of nature with its vivid changes, might be living things capable of determining conviction and prejudice

Figure 297. *"Various Circles," 1926 by Wassili
Kandinsky (1866–1944). The Solomon R.
Guggenheim Museum, New York.*

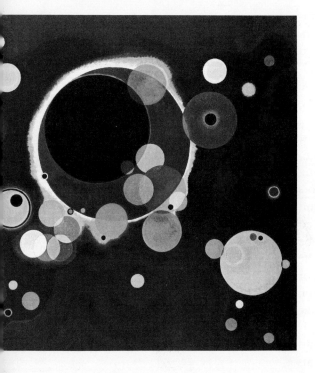

Figure 298. *Brilliant evening dress with evanescent, soap-bubble embroidery was directly inspired by the preceding Kandinsky painting. From
the 1967 collection of the Fontana Sisters. Courtesy of the designer.*

—which always condition the life of man. They discovered that the green chrysoberyl became red with a tangent light and that the amethyst was made of layers of blue and red; and they believed that the opal had stolen its delicate color from the moon. These beliefs of some pushed others into imitations and created legends, traditions, and customs. The jewels, which originated as amulets with different qualities and colors of stones, became obligatory ornaments for deities and for sovereigns of all periods. Thus we see instruments of costume making custom. In modern practice, all of that tradition becomes a complement to clothing and makes its contribution to fashion.

The Russian artist, Wassili Kandinsky, was a high exponent of abstractionism and linked it to a musical structure in pure lines and colors, without subjects. For him the internal melody became a painting, and beauty was an end in itself (Figure 297). The influence of Kandinsky on the young artists of today is greater than it was in his time; his paintings inspire experimental attitudes for the expressive production of works of art and also for applications in costume. Many designs with large and small circles, three-dimensional effects, dots, shadows, and cloudy effects, as seen in the finest chiffons in the official collections of the last three years, were directly inspired by Kandinsky. To *haute couture* he revealed a fine abstract world of grace and color (Figure 298).

Beardsley inspired the couturiers when Courrèges, proposing a black and white totality, bored and brought to a halt the general fantasy. Beardsley's black and white world was chic but not tiring; living, on the contrary, because of its capricious details and mysterious imagery. It has stimulated new ideas in line, in fabric design, in decorations, hairstyles, jewels, and advertising art. His influence, in fact, has invaded every field as a style and a new taste (Figures 299; 300a, b; 301a, b).

Figure 299. *Large shows of Aubrey Beardsley's graphic designs in 1966 and 1967 rekindled interest in a world of sinuous line and black and white fantasy. Here a model in a white organdy cape and lace dress by George Halley stands before a huge reproduction of Beardsley's* Pierrot. *From* Life *magazine, February 24, 1967. Greene-Eula Photo.*

Figure 300. *Beardsley inspires the young designers: two striking silhouettes represent a study for fabric design by Patrizia Sleiter.*

History of Fashions

Figure 301. (a) The Wedding Party *is a humorous rendition of the "black in fashion" in 1963 by Anna Evangelisti. From* Bellezza, *April 1963. Courtesy of the artist.* (b) *A black and white design by Brunetta, who inscribes it: "The models that make the fashions of 1968 stride on."*

a

b

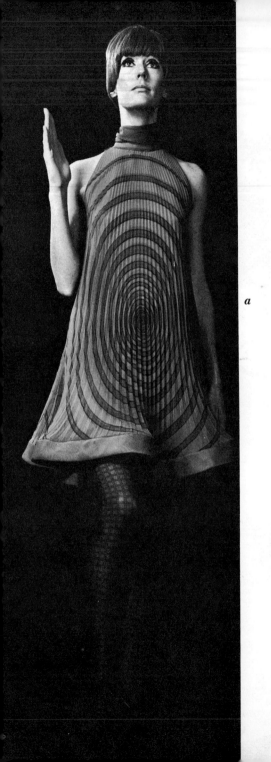

a

b

c

Figure 302. *Two models by Pierre Cardin represent contrasting directions in the recent 1968 fashion world. (a) The mini-gown is youth triumphant. For Cardin, Taroni created this striking fabric with a pinwheel motif—obviously inspired by "Op" art. (b) In contrast, there is a reappearance of the lush, overblown, slightly decadent style of the "twenties." Courtesy of the designer. Two models from the 1969–1970 Autumn/Winter collections. (c) The "Russian Collection" of Jean Baptiste Caumont shows bi-sex styles of full trousers, tops, and lavish furs. Photo by Bob Krieger, Milan. (d) An après-ski outfit by Ken Scott consists of soft, wide jersey trousers and a tabard tunic over a sheer blouse; a jerkin of velvet lined with lapin wards off the cold. Courtesy of the designers.*

d

The Swiss artist Paul Klee was one of that group of "gothic" men who were pervaded by a mysterious pathos—a nostalgia for the primitive or childlike soul. They found insufficient for expressive needs those images presented by the actual world. From the inorganic, enigmatic world, Klee drew new inspiration and left us fresh and fantastic images. We can see also his pervasive influence in modern fashion designs: a different taste in lines, fabrics, colors, and contrasting effects.

Looking at the fashion of today we can see how closely tied it is to art and to culture; and we believe that this adherence gives it value, which assures its position in the history of fashions (Figures 302a–d). One example of the socializing nature of costume is the widespread appearance of fashion reporting in the general press. The late editor of Rome's *Harper's Bazaar*, Irene Brin, did much to contribute to the acceptance of fashion "columns" through her sensitive and humorous articles.

Figure 303. Exciting example of pure art which has effect upon the costume. (*a*) A painting, Mutazioni, *by Achille Perilli.* (*b*) Mutazioni *used as a set and design for costumes in the ballet, of the same name presented at La Scala in Milan.*

a

b

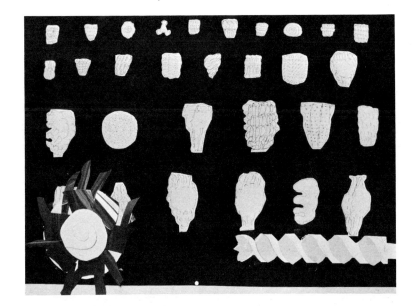

Figure 304. *Design for the costumes of Mozart's "Don Giovanni" by Pietro Consagra, a sculptor. This modern production used mechanized sculptures as the protagonists with the result that costume and set are more strictly tied to each other. Don Giovanni is represented by the large circular form in the lower left corner and the Commander by the long horizontal figure on the right. Courtesy of the artist.*

The study of costume must be considered not only because of its huge and varied production, but also because it is an expression of values affecting taste, and thereby ethics and civilization. The advent of technology advances human relations; it provides themes of collaboration which break down business barriers and national boundaries, proving the general need of a dialogue between technique and culture.

Costume is a point of convergence between the evolution of man and modern specializations. It is a special form of communication, symbolizing society and epoch. The production of fashion becomes a sort of terminal crossing of many specific activities, a new field for experiment, knowledge, foresight, and intuition. It creates a conversation and contributes to the unity between men of different countries. In this way, costume overcomes the limitations of the handicrafts and industrial production and becomes a cultural achievement (Figures 303a, b; 304; 305).

Figure 305. *An elegant armlet in hammered gold, having the grace of an Etruscan jewel, was created by the well-known painter, Giulio Turcato. Courtesy of the artist.*

The Twentieth Century   307

c

modiglia

Figure 306. *The spiritual elegance of these four women from different epochs of history is representative of the eternal type of aristocratic feminine beauty which art will never ignore and fashion will always glorify.* (a) *Nefertiti, Queen of the Eighteenth Dynasty of Egypt. Berlin Museum.* (b) The Princess of Trebisonde, *by Pisanello. Church of St. Anastasia, Verona. Photograph Andersen.* (c) Portrait of Lunia Czschowska *by Amedeo Modigliani, 1919. Photo Anderson.* (d) *The contemporary high fashion model, Mali, with a suggestive hairstyle by Nino Baldan. Hairdos New York Award for 1969.*

d

Fashion, conceived as an eternal proposal of reformation of traditions, is the creative instrument for the renewal of forms, through which costume diffuses the values of society in the times. Costume comes from various experiences, adapting itself continually to new impulses of fashions, and confirming deep connections between fashion and humanity.

We can say that it is the expression of esthetic and ethic tendencies, but for its realization it needs the intervention of technique. Therefore, costume seems to be a natural bridge between technology and culture. It has a great ethic value because it represents the esthetic shape that humanity finds in the time, and it can be considered a confession of man to history (Figures 306a–d).

Bibliography

Baikie, Rev. James, *The Life of the Ancient East,* Macmillan, New York, 1923.

Barnes, Harry E., *An Intellectual and Cultural History of the Western World,* The Cordon Co., Inc., 1937.

Bentivegna, F., *Abbigliamento e Costume nella Pittura Italiana,* C. Bestetti, Rome, 1964.

Boucher, Francois, *A History of Costume in the West,* Thames and Hudson, London, 1967 (English translation of French edition, Flammarion, Paris, 1965).

Brin, Irene, *Usi e Costume: 1920–1940,* Donatello De Luigi, Rome, 1944.

Carra, M., *Dai Nuraghi agli Etruschi,* Fabbri, Milan, 1966.

Childe, V. Gordon, *What Happened in History,* Penguin Books, Harmondsworth, Middlesex, 1961.

Coarelli, F., *L'Oreficeria nell'Arte Classica,* Fabbri, Milan, 1966.

Contini, M., *La Moda nei Secoli,* Mondadori, Milan, 1965.

Davenport, Millia, *The Book of Costume,* Crown, New York, 1962.

Durant, W., *The Story of Civilization,* A. Mondadori, Milan, 1958.

Enciclopedia dello Spettacolo, Sansori, Florence–Rome, 1958.

Evans, Joan, *Dress in Medieval France,* Clarendon Press, Oxford, 1952.

Fiocco A., *Teatro Universale dalle origini a Shakespeare,* Cappelli, Bologna, 1961.

Franco, F. and Reggiori F., *Le Meraviglie del Passato,* A. Mondadori, Milan, 1958.

Frankfort, Henri, *The Birth of Civilization in the Near East,* Indiana University Press, Bloomington, 1954.

———, *Sculpture of the Third Millennium* B.C. *from Tell Asmar and Khafaje,* The University of Chicago Press, Chicago, 1939.

Hope, Thomas, *Costumes of the Greeks and Romans,* Dover, New York, 1962.

Houston, Mary G., *Ancient Egyptian, Mesopotamian and Persian Costume and Decoration,* Second edition, A. and C. Black, London, 1954.

———, *Ancient Greek, Roman and Byzantine Costume and Decoration,* A. and C. Black, London, 1931.

———, *Medieval Costume in England and France, the Thirteenth, Fourteenth and Fifteenth Centuries,* A. and C. Black, London, 1939.

Leloir, M., *Histoire du Costume,* Ernst, Paris, 1933.

Levi, Pisetzky R., *Storia del Costume in Italia,* Istituto Editoriale Italiano, Milan, 1964.

Lloyd, Seton, *The Art of the Ancient Near East,* Praeger, New York, 1961.

Moscati, Sabatino, *The Face of the Ancient Orient,* Vallentine, Mitchell and Co., Ltd., 1960.

Museum of Fine Arts, *Greek, Etruscan and Roman Art,* Boston, 1963.

Nims, Charles F., and Swaan, Wim, *Thebes of the Pharoahs,* Stein and Day, New York, 1965.

Norris, Herbert, *Costume and Fashion,* Dutton, New York, 1924.

Palmer, R., *Mycenaeans and Minoans,* Faber and Faber, London, 1961.

Panzini, A., *La Penultima Moda,* Cremonese ed., Rome, 1930.

Payne, Blanche, *History of Costume,* Harper and Row, New York, 1965.

Pistolese, Rosana, *La Moda nella Storia del Costume,* Capelli, Bologna, 1964.

Piton, C., *Le Costume Civil en France,* E. Flammarion, Paris, 1906.

Planche, James R., *Cyclopaedia of Costume,* Chatto and Winduss, London, 1876, 2 vols.

Richter, Gisela, *Red Figured Athenian Vases in the Metropolitan Museum of Art,* Yale University Press, New Haven, 1936, 2 vols.

————, *The Sculpture and Sculptors of the Greeks,* Yale University Press, New Haven, 1950.

Schafer, H. and Andreae, W., *Die Kunst des Altes Orients,* Proplaen Verlag, Berlin, 1925.

Scheffer, T. V., *Die Kultur der Griechen,* Phaidon Verlag, Vienna, 1935.

Serra, M., *Il Secolo coi Baffi,* Cappelli, Bologna, 1965.

Toschi, P., *Le Origini del Teatro Italiano,* Einaudi, 1955.

Vocino, M., *Storia del Costume,* Libreria dello Stato, Rome, 1952.

Zehren, Erich, *The Crescent and the Bull,* Hawthorn Books, Inc., New York, 1962.

Glossary of Foreign Words

Academos—(Gr.) The Academy in the suburbs of Athens where Plato taught.

Aigrette—(Fr.) Plume or tuft of feathers used to decorate coiffure or hat.

À la Française—(Fr.) In the French fashion.

À la Frangipane—(Fr.) Perfume used to scent gloves; a style launched by the Marquis de Frangipane.

À la Grecque—(Fr.) In the Greek fashion.

À la Victime—(Fr.) A fad after the French Revolution of tying a red ribbon around the neck, recalling the victims of the guillotine.

All' Italiana—(It.) In the Italian fashion.

Anaxirides—(Gr.) Long, bloused trousers worn by Persians.

Apoptygma—(Gr.) The draped and pendent folds of a Greek tunic.

Aumônière—(Fr.) A little alms purse first worn by the Crusaders.

315

Balzo—(It.) Elaborate Italian hat of the Fifteenth Century.

Barbette—(Fr.) A linen covering for the throat; a women's fashion adapted by religious orders.

Barocco—(It.) Baroque style of the Seventeenth Century characterized by extremes, or irregularities, of form.

Basque—(Fr.) Part of a costume—skirt, flaps, or tail—that falls from the waist downward.

Bauta—(It.) A black silk or lace veil worn by Venetian ladies during the Eighteenth Century.

Belle Epoque—(Fr.) A period at the end of the Nineteenth Century characterized by gaiety and frivolity.

Bizarrerie—(Fr.) Eccentricity; whimsy.

Bouillonè—(Fr.) A padded or stuffed trimming for armholes.

Boutique—(Fr.) A shop, often for specialties of costume.

Brassière—(Fr.) A bodice, vest, or light jacket.

Byzantine—(Lat.) An overdress with embroidered sleeves, so-called for its Oriental flavor.

Buskins—(Origin doubtful) Greek sandals with high cork soles.

Cache-Enfant—(Fr.) A padded overskirt with high waistline in fashion during the Seventeenth Century.

Café-Chantant—(Fr.) Café with evening entertainment.

Canepin—(Fr.) A thin, soft leather used for gloves or in the construction of wigs.

Capote—(Fr.) After 1870: a little hat decorated with flowers and plumes; originally signified a coat with a hood.

Caraco—(Fr.) A ladies' jacket of Spanish origin worn in the late Eighteenth Century.

Carmagnole—(Fr.) Men's short jacket adopted during the French Revolution.

Casula—(Lat.) Originally a robe that enclosed the body like a box. Later it became a short, straight garment and finally was worn only be ecclesiastics.

Centunculos—(Lat.) A padded doublet worn by actors in Greek and Roman comedy.

Chlaina—(Gr.) Short mantle of the Greeks; sometimes draped about the hips as an overskirt by the ladies.

Chapeau à Bavolet—(Fr.) Attractive Nineteenth Century adaptation of a peasant's bonnet with ruffle covering the nape of the neck.

Chaperon—(Fr.) A draped headcovering for men worn from the Twelfth Century until the Sixteenth.

Chiaroscuro—(Ital.) Strong contrast in the arrangement of light and shade as practiced by Baroque artists.

Chiton—(Gr.) The basic tunic of ancient Greece worn by both men and women.

Chlamys—(Gr.) A short oblong mantle worn by horsemen in ancient Greece; later, generally adopted for outdoor wear.

Clavus—(Lat.) A vertical purple stripe of varying width worn on tunics by Roman senators and knights as a symbol of rank.

Cloche—(Fr.) A bell-shaped hat of felt for women.

Coiffe—(Fr.) A term designating various headcoverings for women, usually made of linen.

Coiffure à la Sévigné or **en Bouffons**—(Fr.) A coiffure arranged with two bunches of curls at sides of head, made famous by Mme. de Sévigné.

Coiffure à la Titus—(Fr.) Hair cut very short, gamin-like; a style popular in 1793.

Coiffure en Corymbe—(Fr.) Mythological hairstyle resembling a cluster of fruit or flowers.

Coiffure en Fontanges—(Fr.) So-called after Mlle de Fontanges; the hair was tied on top of the head and surmounted by a stiffened lace ruffle attached to a round bonnet.

Coiffure en Hérisson—(Fr.) An Eighteenth Century hairstyle arranged in a palisade of spikes on top of the head, garnished with ribbons and plumes.

Coiffure en Hurluberlu—(Fr.) Hair curled tightly and massed in two great bunches with long pendent curls; worn in the Seventeenth Century.

Coiffure en Oreilles de Chien—(Fr.) Hairstyle resembling ears of a spaniel adopted by the Incroyables of the Directoire.

Coiffure en Serpenteau—(Fr.) Hairstyle composed of long serpentine curls popular early in the reign of Louis XIV.

Coiffure en Tête—(Fr.) Elaborate Renaissance hairstyle composed with feathers and jewels.

Commedia Dell'Arte—(Ital.) Theater of stock characters and plots that developed in Sixteenth Century Italy.

Commedia di Costume—(Ital.) Theatrical innovation of the Eighteenth Century.

Conque—(Fr.) A shell-shaped coiffe, stiffened with wires, worn by women in mourning in the Seventeenth Century.

Coram Populo—(Lat.) Adverb meaning in front of everybody, in public; a type of toga worn by victorious generals in ancient Rome.

Cornette—(Fr.) A type of coiffe folded so as to make horns at the upper sides of the head.

Cotardie—(Ital.) A surcoat or overdress of varied forms that was widely adopted in the Fourteenth Century.

Cotta—(Ital.) Surplice worn over armor by the Crusaders.

Cravat à la Steinkerque—(Fr.) Long cravat of batiste usually trimmed with lace; it was wrapped casually around the neck and loosely knotted.

Crespine—(Fr.) A gold net for retaining the hair used by ladies in the Middle Ages.

Crinoline—(Fr.) A petticoat stiffened with horsehair to support the wide skirts of mid-Nineteenth Century.

Cucullus—(Lat.) A hood worn by monks; the hood of the Roman traveling cloak.

Cul de Paris or **Faux Cul**—(Fr.) A small cushion of horsehair that formed a little bustle in Eighteenth Century dresses.

Dactyliothecae—(Lat.) Collections of antique jewelry.

Dalmatic—(Lat.) A loose super tunic (imported to Rome from Dalmatia) worn by early Christians and, later, by ecclesiastics.

Demi-Ceint—(Fr.) A narrow belt or chain with pendent decorations, important addition to the Fourteenth Century gown.

Dentelles—(Fr.) Borders or bands of lace.

Déshabillé-Négligé—(Fr.) Boudoir wrap; at-home gown.

Dessous—(Fr.) Undergarments.

Dolce Stil Novo—(Ital.) Sweet new style of poetry initiated by Dante.

Dorelots—(Fr.) A short curly hairstyle worn with coiffe by men in the Middle Ages.

Duecento—(Ital.) The Thirteenth Century.

Entrave—(Fr.) A ribbon tied below the knees created the hobble skirt of 1912.

Ephod—(Heb.) The Hebrew overdress and religious garment.

Étoffes à Miroirs—(Fr.) Eighteenth Century taffeta fabric worked in squares.

Falbalas—(Fr.) Bands of pleated or gathered material that form loose ruffles.

Fard—(Fr.) Heavy tinted make-up used in the Eighteenth Century.

Ferronière—(Fr.) Chain with jewel worn on the coiffure, stylish in the time of Louis XVIII.

Fêtes Galantes—(Fr.) Gay parties or entertainments.

Fichu—(Fr.) A softly draped collar of light cotton or mousseline de soie.

Filet—(Fr.) Fine thread.

Fin de Siècle—(Fr.) End of the Century.

Flammeum—(Lat.) Flame-colored bridal veil of ancient Rome.

Frac—(Fr.) A man's double-breasted coat with long skirts or tails.

Furies—(Fr.) Multicolored cottons from India popular in the Eighteenth Century.

Garland or **Ghirlanda**—(Ital.) Fifteenth Century head-dress composed of wreath of flowers, leaves, or peacock feathers.

Genre (painting)—(Fr.) Paintings of common subjects that illustrate the manners, fashions, or taste of a period.

Gilet—(Fr.) A sleeveless waistcoat or vest that derived its name from Gilles, a French comic actor of the Nineteenth Century.

Giornea—(Ital.) Fifteenth Century ladies' cloak.

Godet—(Fr.) A flare or gore inserted in skirts.

Gonella—(Ital.) Short tunic worn under the guarnacca.

Gotico Fiorito or **International Gothic**—(Ital.) A style of art emphasizing linear elegance and naturalistic detail that flourished in the late Fourteenth Century.

Gourgandine—(Fr.) A laced corset without bones worn under the peignoir of the Seventeenth Century.

Guarnacca—(Ital.) Long tunic or robe worn by men of letters from the Thirteenth Century.

Guimpe—(Fr.) A starched voile or lace covering for throat, shoulders and, often, chin and temples as well.

Hennin—(Fr.) A long, cone-shaped head-dress, usually with pendent veil worn by women in the Fifteenth Century.

Himation—(Gr.) The long, rectangular cloak worn by both sexes in ancient Greece.

Houppe—(Fr.) Tuft of feathers attached to the front of the forehead and worn with a veil for mourning in Seventeenth Century Netherlands.

Huiken—(Fr.) Long, pleated veil-cloak worn in Netherlands in the Seventeenth Century.

Impasse—(Fr.) Dilemma.

Incroyables—(Fr.) Nickname given to the dandies of the Directoire.

Intermezzo—(Ital.) Musical interlude performed between acts of a play in Sixteenth and Seventeenth Centuries.

Joie de Vivre—(Fr.) Joy of life; exhiliration.

Jus—(Lat.) Law; legal principle, right, or power.

Justaucorp à Brevet—(Fr.) Elegant waistcoat bestowed on privileged courtiers by Louis XIV.

Kaftan—(Turk.) Hebrew overdress for traveling.

Kalasyris—(Gr.) A long sheath, but also a pleated and draped dress, worn in ancient Egypt.

Kitonet—(Gr.) Wrapped skirt of the Phoenicians.

Klaft—(Copt.) Draped headcovering of upper class in ancient Egypt.

Kolbak or **Colback**—(Fr.) Tall Russian-style hat of fur, sometimes worn with military dress uniform.

Kylix—(Gr.) A stemmed drinking cup with shallow bowl and two handles.

Kystae—(Gr.) Etruscan cosmetic case of bronze.

Lacerna—(Lat.) Roman mantle for cold weather.

Lattuga—(Ital.) Ruff, band, or jabot gathered and curled like a lettuce leaf.

Liaisons Amoureuses—(Fr.) Amorous attachments.

Manchette—(Fr.) Cuff or ruffle at the wristband of a chemise or dress.

Mecenatismo—(Ital.) A system of patronage, protection.

Merveilleuse—(Fr.) Liberated woman of the Directoire.

Mise en Scène—(Fr.) Staged spectacle.

Mitaines—(Fr.) Mittens; gloves made without complete fingers.

Mondaines—(Fr.) Worldly women of fashion.

Novecento—(Ital.) The Twentieth Century.

Onkos—(Gr.) A special hairstyle used in Greek and Roman theater.

Paenula—(Lat.) Heavy Roman traveling cape of wool, felt, or leather.

Palazzi—(Ital.) Palaces; mansions.

Palla—(Lat.) The veil or cloak worn over the tunic by women of ancient Rome.

Panaches—(Fr.) Flourishing plumes worn on hat or coiffure, especially in the Seventeenth Century.

Panier—(Fr.) Hooped petticoat or framework under skirt that created many changes of silhouette in the Eighteenth Century.

Panno d'Oro—(Ital.) Soft golden cloth favored for Fourteenth Century gowns.

Panseron—(Fr.) Waistcoat stiffly lined with cardboard worn at end of the Sixteenth Century.

Pavane—(Fr.) Grave, stately dance from the Spanish court.

Pèlerine—(Fr.) Cape covering just the shoulders.

Pellanda—(Lat.) Ample tunic with cowl.

Perruque à la Brigadière—(Fr.) Simple, military-style wig of the Seventeenth Century.

Perruque à Fenêtres—(Fr.) Type of wig worn by Louis XIV so that he could blend and augment his natural hair with false hair.

Perruque en Folio—(Fr.) Huge and heavy wig, worn during Louis XIV's reign.

Petite Oie—(Fr.) Decorative trimming of little curled ribbons popularized by courtiers under Louis XIV.

Pièce d'Estomac—(Fr.) A ruffled or embroidered triangular piece of material inserted in front of bodice in Seventeenth Century dresses.

Pied d'Ours—(Fr.) A shoe resembling a bear's paw from early Sixteenth Century.

Pistagna—(Ital.) A faced collar on the scapular worn by knights in the Middle Ages.

Plissé—(Fr.) A pleated dress.

Polis—(Gr.) The city-state of ancient Greece.

Pompons—(Fr.) Ornamental tuft or tassel.

Pouf—(Fr.) A skirt arranged in soft flounces in back; a variation of the tournure popular in late Nineteenth Century.

Princesse—(Fr.) Fitted dress with natural lines.

Pschent—The Pharoah's Crown of Egypt worn after the unification of the North and South Kingdoms.

Pulcinellate—(Ital.) Eighteenth Century paintings interpreting the masks of Commedia dell'Arte.

Putti—(Ital.) Baroque decoration of little cherubs.

Rabat—(Fr.) A turned collar of lace, or linen trimmed with lace, worn by men in the Seventeenth Century.

Res Publica—(Lat.) Commonweal; state.

Réticule—(Fr.) Small handbag of silk or of gold net.

Rhingrave—(Fr.) Petticoat breeches; an effeminate fashion popular with men of the mid-Seventeenth Century.

Robe à l'Anglaise—(Fr.) Dress in the English fashion; jacket and soft skirt worn over small bustle in the late Eighteenth Century.

Robe Battante also called **Robe à la Watteau**—(Fr.) Early Eighteenth Century gown with graceful pleats hanging from shoulders.

Robe en Chemise—(Fr.) Long, loose, shirt-like dress of mousseline worn in late Eighteenth Century.

Robe de Chambre—(Fr.) Loose, casual at-home gown for men and women.

Robe Manteau—(Fr.) A dress with the styling of a cloak.

Robe à Tournure Strapontin—(Fr.) Fashion of 1886 draped fullness of skirt in the rear over an exaggerated bustle.

Rocaille—(Fr.) An exaggeration of the Rococo style using shells and rocks in light, decorative manner.

Rococo—(Fr.) Eighteenth Century artistic style marked by fanciful use of light, curvilinear forms, gay ornamentation, often mythological subject matter.

Rodin—(Fr.) Wood from India used for canes in Eighteenth Century.

Roi Soleil—(Fr.) Louis the XIV, the "Sun King".

Romanity—(Ital.) The spirit or essence of Rome.

Rouleau-Cliché—(Fr.) Roller with raised designs for printing textiles, invented in 1775.

Sagus—(Lat.) The Byzantine cloak.

Sarmat—(Lat.) A Phoenician hat that protected the ears.

Scapular—(Lat.) Sleeveless outer garment, short or long, sometimes with a cowl, worn by knights and ecclesiastics.

Scarsella—(Ital.) Ladies' small purse that hung from the belt, used in the Middle Ages.

Seicento—(Ital.) The Seventeenth Century.

Skent—Short, wrap-around skirt worn by early Egyptian men.

Soubrette—(Fr.) Coquettish waitress, ingenue.

Spencer—Very short jacket in broadcloth or velvet, with long, fitted sleeves adapted by ladies in early Nineteenth Century from English style of Lord Spencer.

Spira—(Gr.) Coiffure used in Crete, Greece, and Rome in which the hair was coiled into long curls and held in place with a band.

Tabarro—(Ital.) Venetian cloak with pèlerine worn in early Eighteenth Century.

Tablion—(Lat.) Rectangular patch, heavily embroidered, that ornamented the cloak of Byzantine dignitaries.

Taffetas—(Fr.) A light, crisp fabric introduced in the Fifteenth Century.

Tailleur—(Fr.) The tailored suit for women first introduced at end of Nineteenth Century.

Tapissier—(Fr.) Tapestry-maker.

Tassello—(Ital.) A piece of lace inserted in the low neckline of Fourteenth Century dresses.

Tebenna—(Lat.) The Etruscan mantle, horse-shoe shaped for dancers.

Ténèbres—(Fr.) Small, black scarf worn on the coiffure en Fontanges.

Thirsus—(Gr.) Staff carried by maenads and bacchants in Greek painting.

Toga—(Lat.) The Roman cloak.

Toga Atra or **Sordida**—(Lat.) Black toga worn for mourning.

Toga Bastarda—(Lat.) An assymetrical tunic worn in the Roman theater.

Toga Candida—(Lat.) White toga worn by aspirants for public office.

Toga Picta—(Lat.) Toga of fine, purple cloth bordered with gold palms signifying victory.

Toga Praetexta—(Lat.) White toga with purple border worn by governing officials.

Toga Trabea—(Lat.) Purple toga with train worn by the Augures.

Toga Virilis—(Lat.) Commonly used toga in rough wool.

Toga Vitrea—(Lat.) A transparent voile toga worn by effeminate men.

Toque—(Fr.) Hat of Spanish origin popular in Sixteenth Century.

Tour Merlons—(Fr.) The crenellations seen in a fortification; notched trimming on garments of the Middle Ages.

Touret—(Fr.) Coiffe with voile covering sides of head and throat introduced in Fourteenth Century.

Tournure—(Fr.) Style introduced by Queen Victoria in which the skirt was draped in the rear over a bustle.

Trapèze—(Fr.) Dress with trapezoidal skirt.

Trecento—(Ital.) The Fourteenth Century.

Trompe-l'Oeil—(Fr.) Illusion; deceptive appearance of reality.

Trousse—(Fr.) Short, voluminous breeches with vertical slashes.

Troussoir—(Fr.) A jeweled hook for carrying the trains of dresses.

Truffeau—(Fr.) Ladies' hat composed with rolls of false hair worn in Fourteenth and Fifteenth Centuries.

Tunica Palmata—(Lat.) Tunic embroidered with golden palms.

Uraeus—(Lat.) Sacred asp; symbol of sovereignty in ancient Egypt.

Vair—(Fr.) Gray and white fur lining of cloaks and robes in Middle Ages.

Vertugadin—(Fr.) Hoop-skirt of the Seventeenth Century.

Vertugadin a Tambour—(Fr.) Hoop-skirt in the shape of a drum.

Volant—(Fr.) Ruffle; light, floating drapery.

Zimarra—(Ital.) Tunic or robe of sumptuous material.

Index

329

Tunics (*continued*)
    pellanda, 146
    Persian, 10
    Roman sleeved, 85
    Sumerian, 2
    zimarra, 133
Turbans, Hebrew, 36
Twentieth Century, 275–310

Universities, 128
Ur, 3

Vair, 144; 145, Fig. 140
Van Dyck, Anthony, 203
Vases
    Cretan, 41
    Etruscan, 72
    Greek, 53
Velasquez, Diego de Silva, 203
Velvet, 143
Vermeer, Jan, 213
Veronese, Paolo, 177
Versailles, 208
Volants
    Cretan, 43

Volants (*continued*)
    falbalas, 215, 216
    Sumerian, 3

Waistcoats
    Eighteenth Century, 236
    gilet, 256
    justaucorp à brevet, 214
    panseron, 184
Waistlines
    empire, 281, Fig. 283
    Fifteenth Century, 157
    waspwaist, 250, Fig. 252
Warriors, Mycenaean, 46, Fig. 35
Watteau, Antoine, 220
Weaving, 36
Wigs
    à la brigadière, 217
    à fenêtres, 209
    en folio, 209
    Egyptian, 29
Wool, 76
    Trojan use, 50
Wooley, C. Leonard, 3

Zimarra, 133